Maxine
YELLING IT LIKE IT IS

Maxine

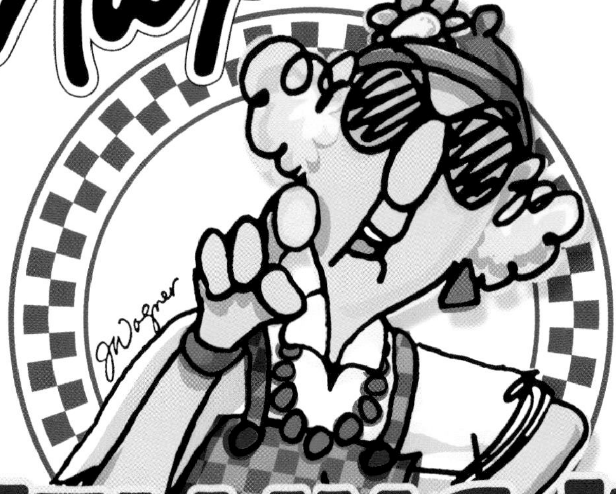

YELLING IT LIKE IT IS

A Fine Whine With the Queen of Attitude

Hallmark BOOKS

STOREY BOOKS

BOK2012

The mission of Storey Communications is to serve our customers by publishing practical information that encourages personal independence in harmony with the environment.

Created by
John M. Wagner

Written by
Dan Taylor

Contributing Writers
Chris Brethwaite
Bill Bridgeman
Russ Ediger
Scott Emmons
Bill Gray
Allyson Jones
Steve King
Mark Oatman
Deeann Stewart
Bill Whitehead
Myra Zirkle

Edited by
Jenise Johnson-Carl

Designed by
Jim Langford
Deb Kitchen

Back cover by
Leslie Constantino

Production by
Erin Lincourt

Produced by Storey Communications, Inc., Schoolhouse Rd., Pownal, VT 05261.

www.maxine.com
www.storeybooks.com

PRINTED IN CHINA
10 9 8 7 6 5 4 3 2 1

Library of Congress Cataloging-in-Publication Data

Maxine yelling it like it is: a fine whine with the queen of attitude / by Maxine.
p. cm.
ISBN 1-58017-391-8 (pbk.)
1. American wit and humor.
PN6162 .M295 2001
741.5'973—dc21 00-053803

CONTENTS

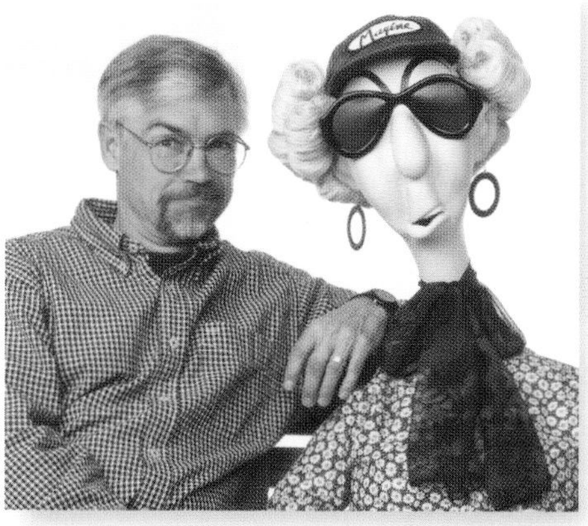
Maxine

To all the women everywhere who have
laughed with Maxine over the past 15 years.

JWagner

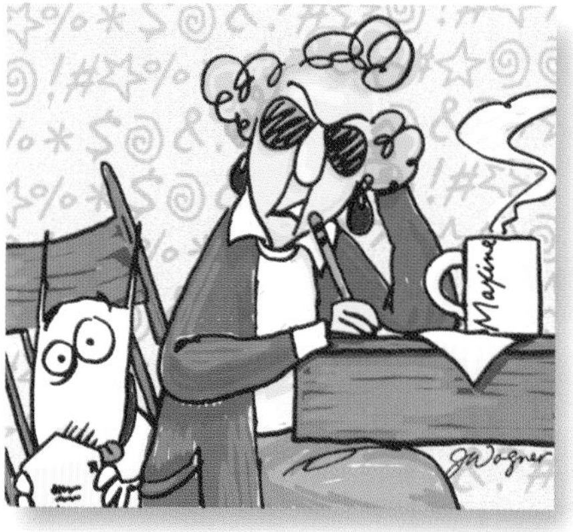
Maxine
JWagner

FOREWORD

Contents:
Pack of lies.

-Maxine

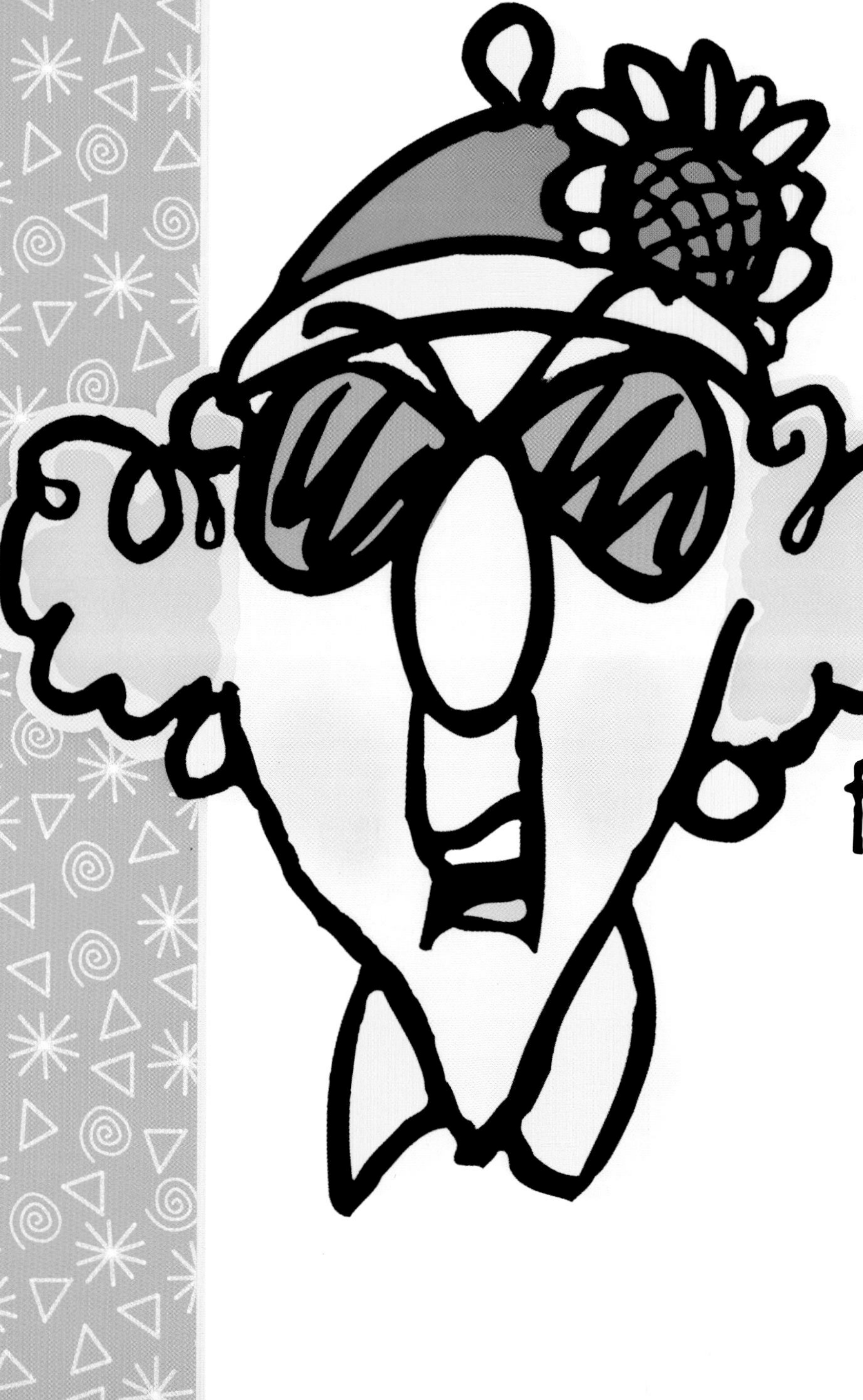

I think
you'll
find
this
fascinating.
I know
I do!

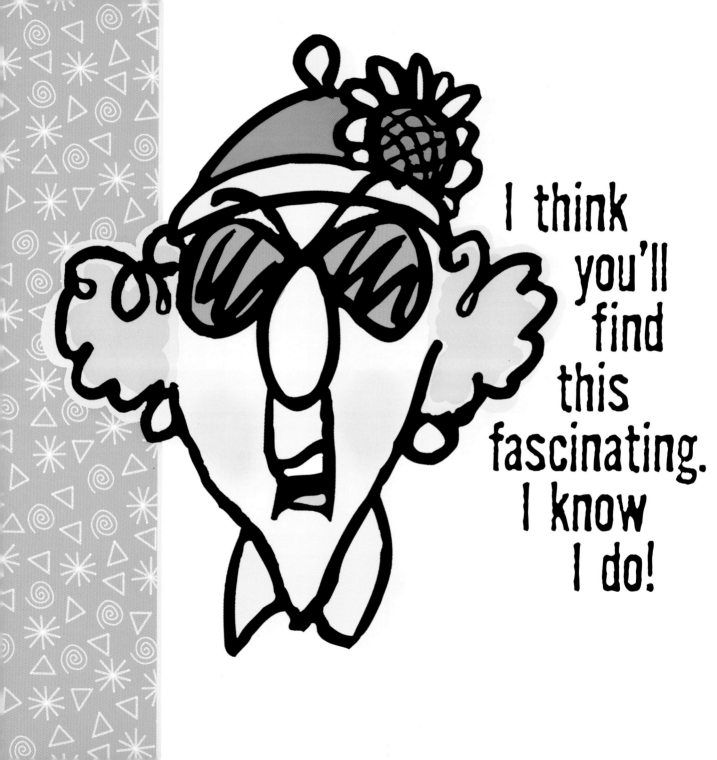

To Know Me Is to... Well, Know Me

YOU KNOW THAT NICE OLDER LADY WHO LIVES DOWN the street and you see tending her cats or maybe cooling a pie on the windowsill? That's not me. Not even close. I don't live on anybody's street—they live on mine. I don't work well in groups, and I don't work at all if I can get away with it. I tell it like it is, and if I don't like how it is, I tell it like it ought to be. And *I'm* my own biggest fan. But you're free to join in the hard-fought fight for second place.

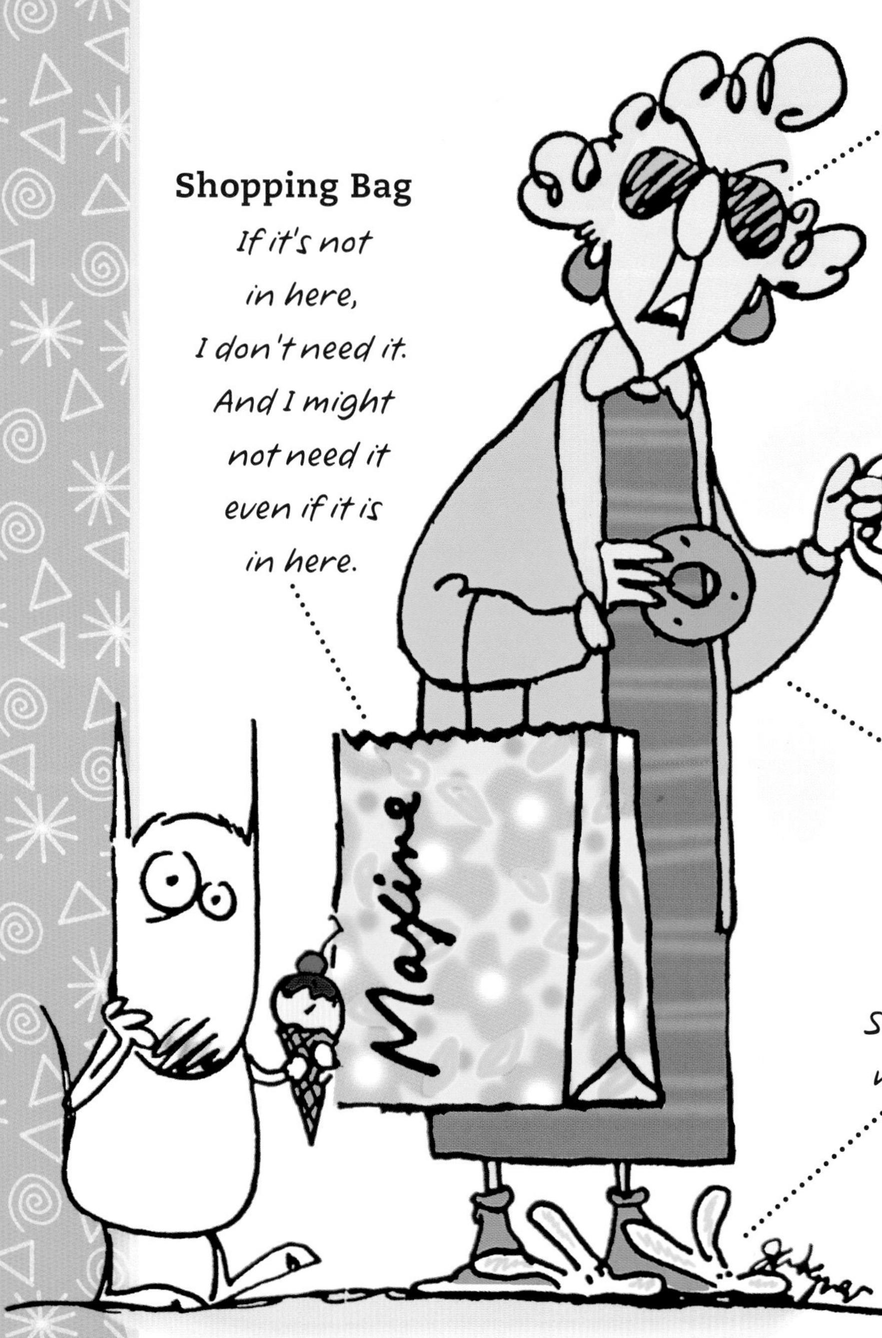
Sunglasses
Make it easier to nod off without... Oh, not that I ever would...
Shopping Bag
If it's not in here, I don't need it. And I might not need it even if it is in here.
Mug
Talk to the mug.
I ♥ MY ATTITUDE PROBLEM
Maxine
Robe
Kick-around-the-house robe. You want to be first?
Bunny Slippers
Shoe shopping is easy when you're looking for "furry" and "flop-eared."

NAME:
What's it to you, pal?

AGE:
Twenty-one, plus a few extra years you don't need to know about.

WEIGHT:
Just heavy enough to kick your butt.

BIRTHDAY:
Last person who guessed won a fat lip.

CURRENT HOME:
Mobile.

OCCUPATION:
Retired, but I do a lot of volunteer griping.

FAVORITE HOBBY:
Collecting coins. Usually from mall fountains.

FAVORITE CHILDHOOD MEMORY:
Learning to ride a two-wheeler...through the neighbor's flower bed.

PERSONAL HEROES:
I have three. Me, myself, and I.

THREE WORDS THAT BEST DESCRIBE YOU:
Leave. Me. Alone.

Maxine:
Up Close and Too Personal

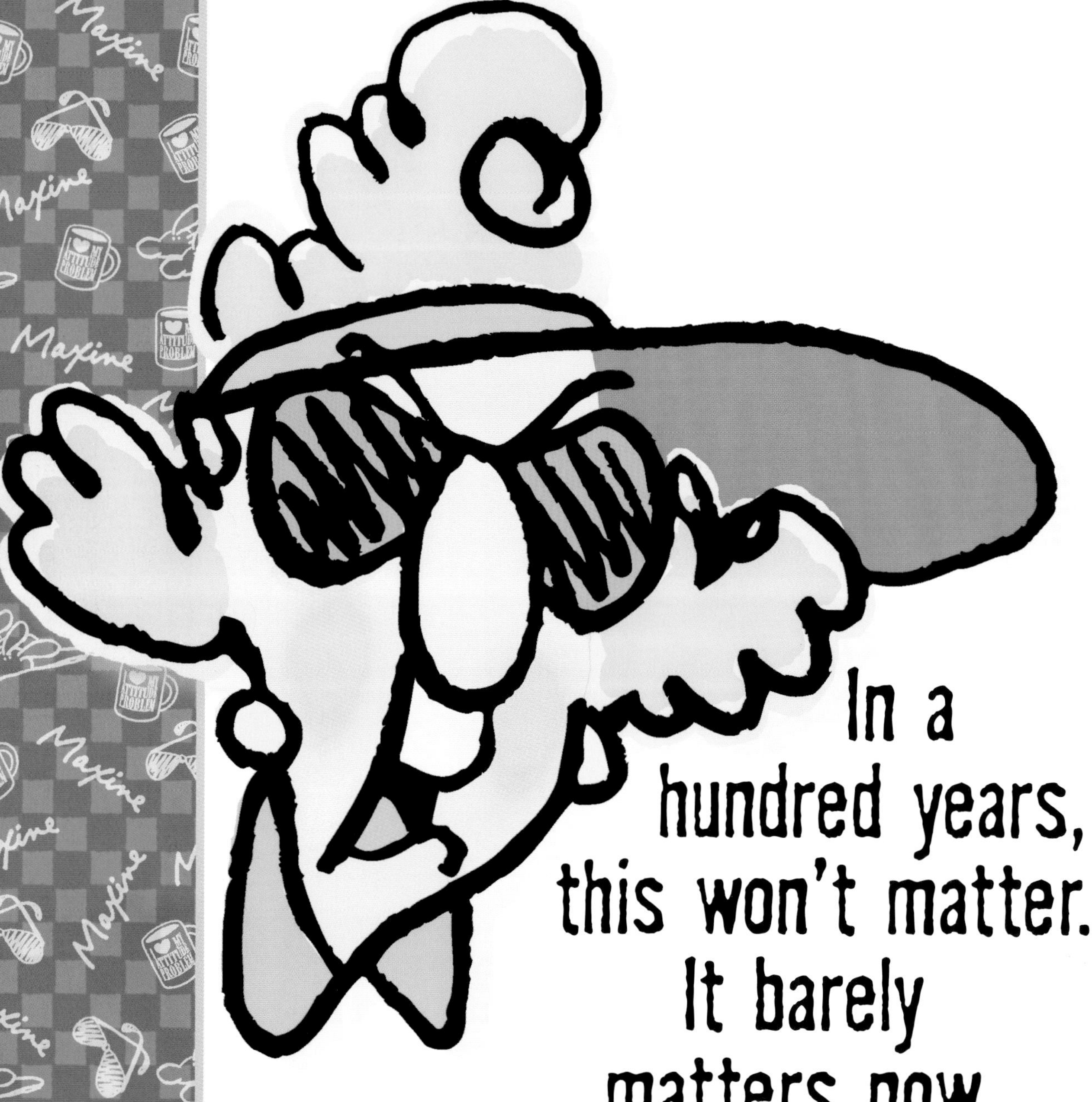

In a
hundred years,
this won't matter.
It barely
matters now.

Maxine: Born to Be Riled

THE YEAR WAS 1986. I REMEMBER IT LIKE IT WAS YESTERDAY. In fact, I remember it better than yesterday, but that's another story. America needed a new voice. A raspy voice that sounded like another coughing fit was just seconds away. A voice that would tell it like it is, shoot from the plastic hip, and cut the crap. That's a lot to ask from a voice, but I'm used to asking for a lot. The time was ripe, and so was John Wagner.

When John first drew me on a greeting card, he couldn't have guessed what kind of rusty can he'd opened, what kind of scratchy cat he'd let out of the bag, what kind of rickety bridge he'd crossed, what kind of...Oh, you see where I'm heading with this.

I began to show up on coffee mugs, just in case the coffee didn't get you jittery enough already. I was immortalized on nutcrackers and cookie jars and even some things that people don't need. Gripers united in the first official fan club in 1999. Like I say, it's better to join a club than get whacked with one.

1986

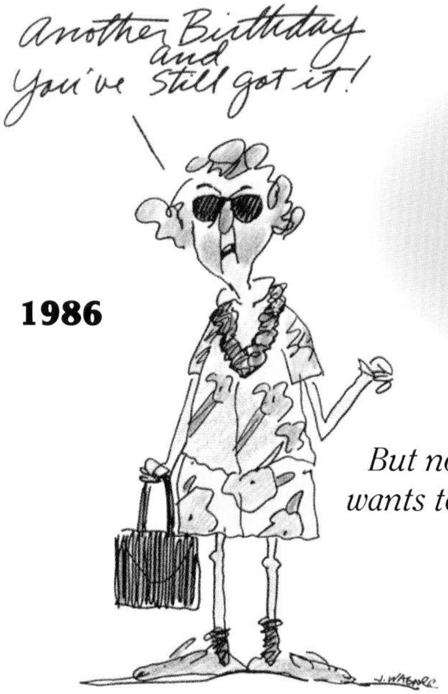
Another Birthday and You've Still got it!

But nobody wants to see it.

Looking back at these greeting cards gives me a warm feeling all over–or maybe it's just the burrito I had for lunch.

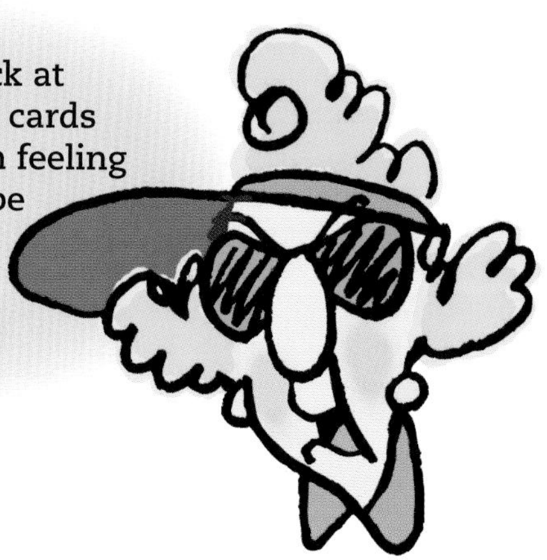

1996

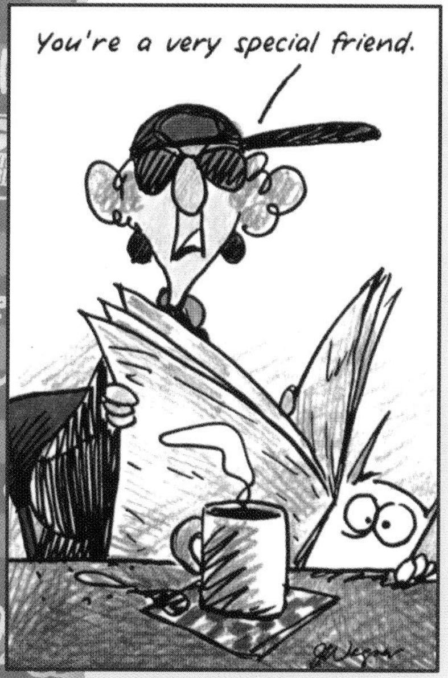
You're a very special friend.

One I actually like.

1991

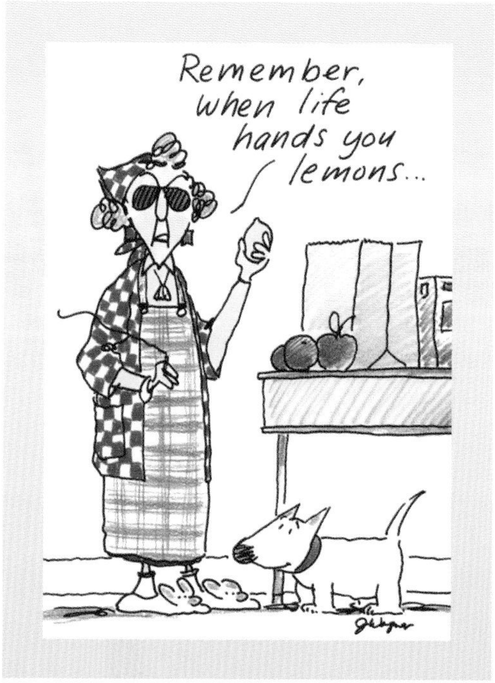
Remember, when life hands you lemons...

...tuck 'em inside your bra! Couldn't hurt. Might help!

2000

Age doesn't make us forgetful.

Having way too many stupid things to remember makes us forgetful.

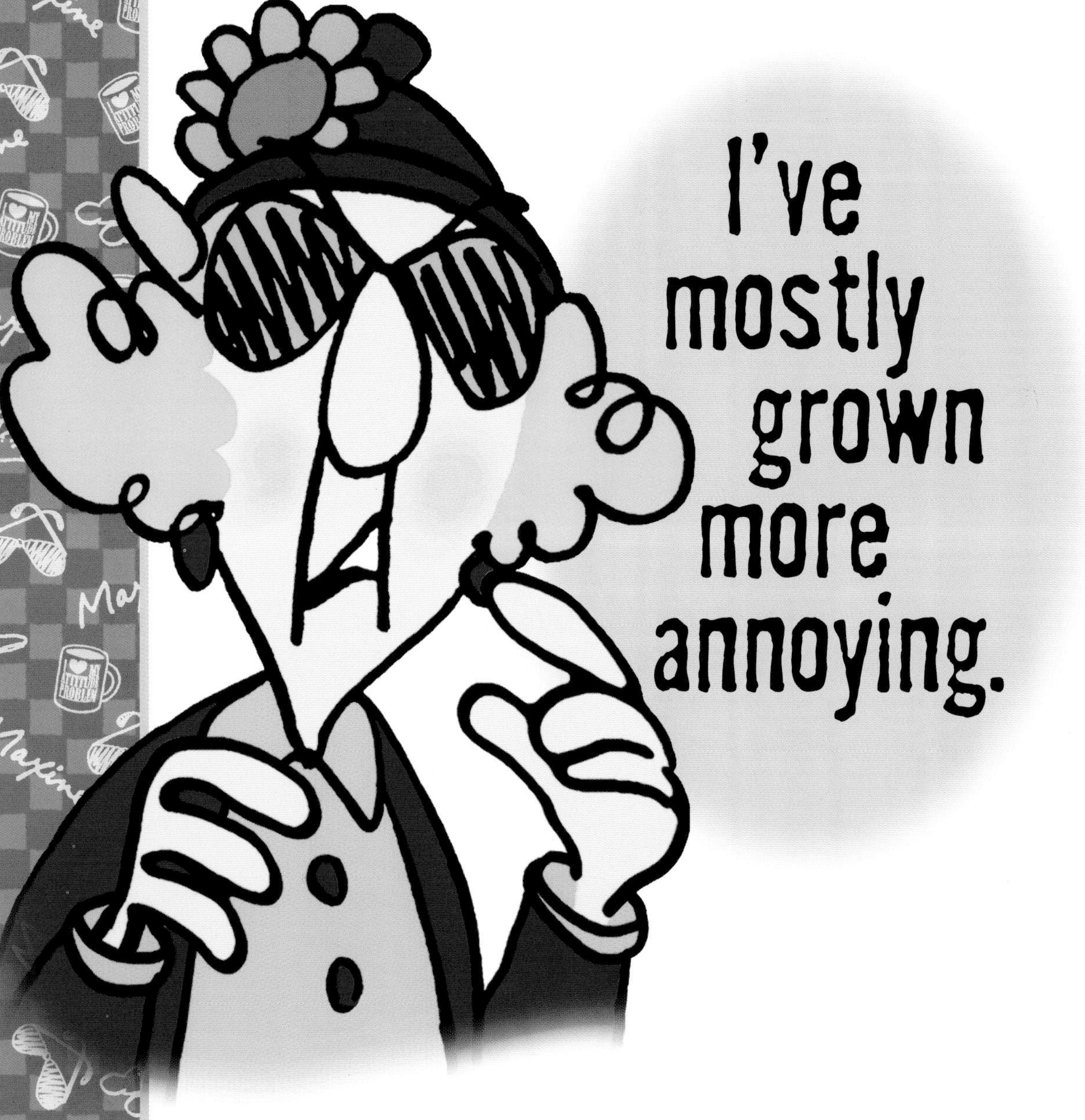
I've mostly grown more annoying.

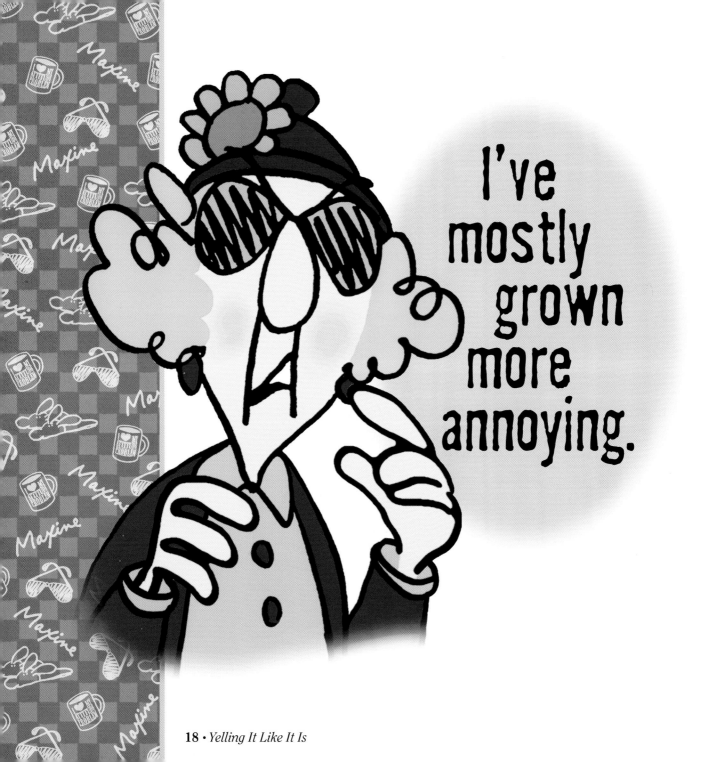

Me in 1986.

Me today.

John drew, the writers wrote, and a legend was born. People loved my attitude problem. America took me to its collective bosom, and it was smothery and smelled of too much perfume. But I knew America meant well, so I let it slide. Soon I was everywhere, like the flu. And also like the flu, I wouldn't go away, no matter what.

An apple
a day
keeps
everyone
away
if your
aim is
good enough.

Another Day, Another Holler

YOU KNOW WHAT BUGS ME? OK, ALMOST EVERYTHING. BUT some things that don't seem so big can really do a water-torture number on your nerves. For example, 12 items is not 13 items. Never will be. If your beeper goes off in a movie theater, you'd better be a brain surgeon. *A famous* brain surgeon. Why do I have to show ID for a check for $12.97? How dumb a criminal would I have to be? You can't walk *onto* the elevator until I get *out of* the elevator. And if I wanted to smell like what "we're sampling today," I would have bought what "we're sampling today."

There are more, oh, lots more. Time and space and constant warnings from my doctor prevent me from going on.

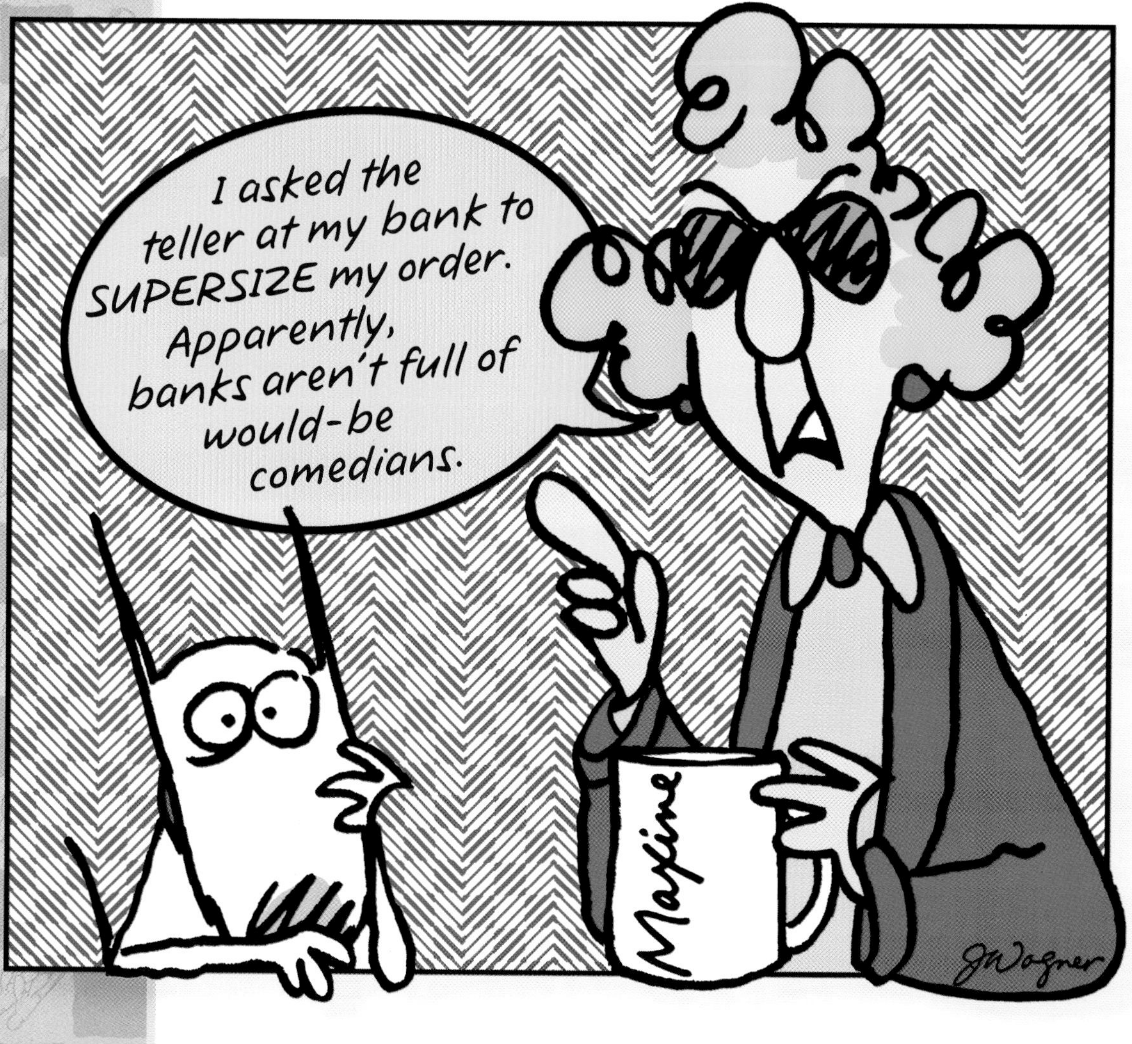
I asked the teller at my bank to SUPERSIZE my order. Apparently, banks aren't full of would-be comedians.
Maxine
JWagner

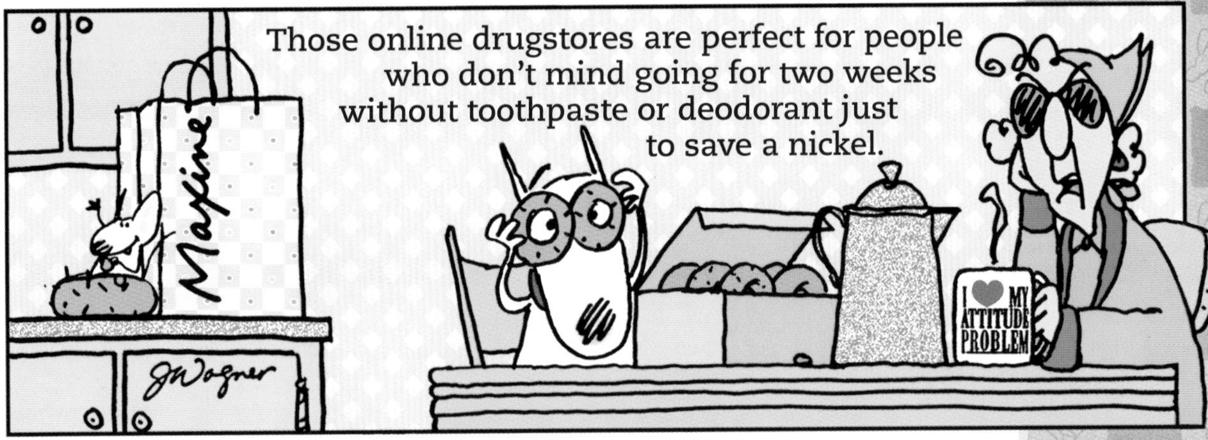
Those online drugstores are perfect for people who don't mind going for two weeks without toothpaste or deodorant just to save a nickel.
Maxine
I ♥ MY ATTITUDE PROBLEM

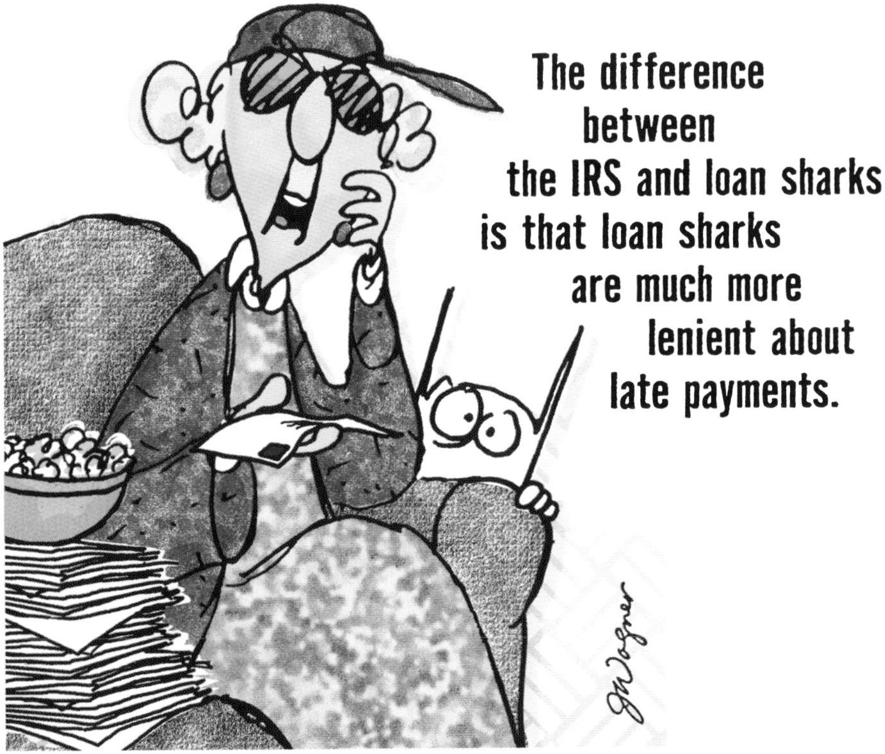
The difference between the IRS and loan sharks is that loan sharks are much more lenient about late payments.

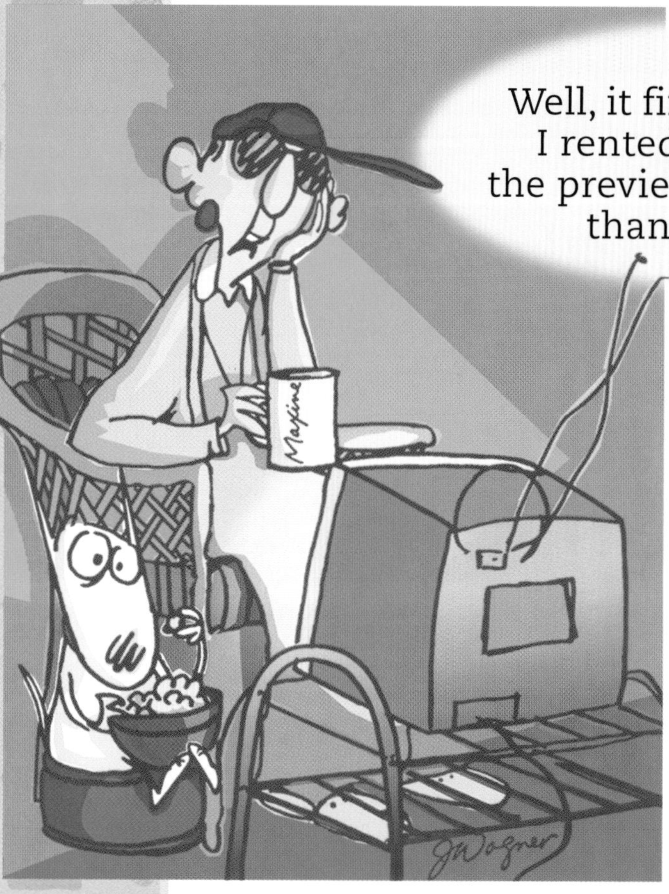
Maxine

Well, it finally happened.
I rented a video, and
the previews were longer
than the movie.

I can't use
a cell phone in the car.
I have to keep
my hands free
for making gestures.

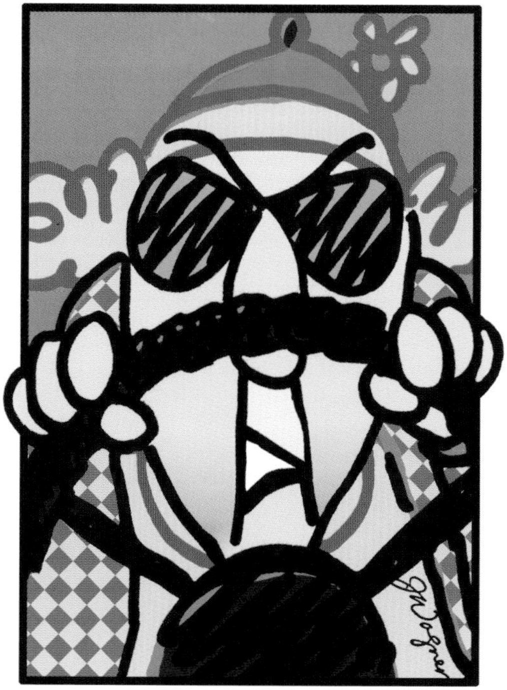

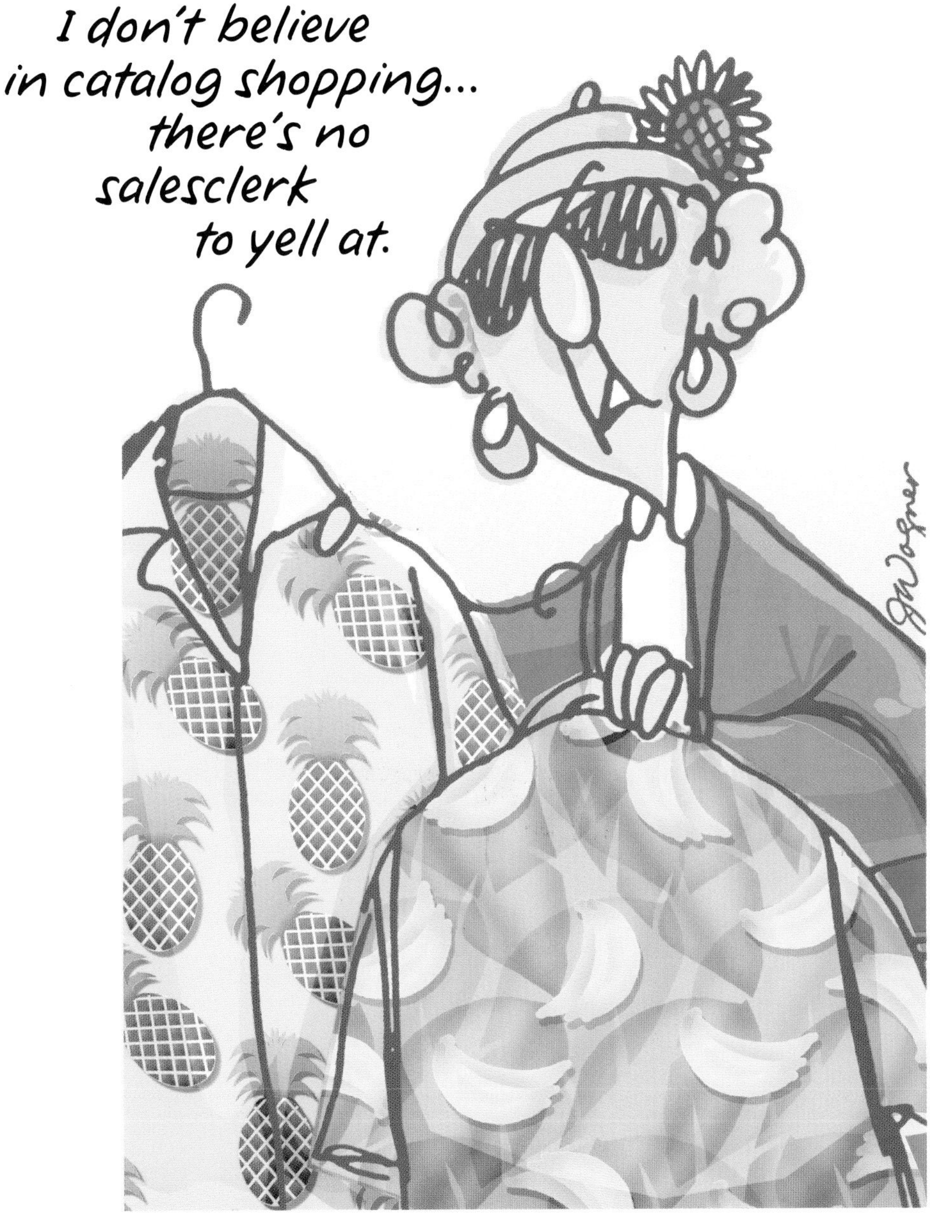
I don't believe
in catalog shopping...
there's no
salesclerk
to yell at.

ONLY TWO THINGS KEEP FLYING FROM BEING A 100 PERCENT PLEASANT EXPERIENCE — the part on the ground and the part in the air.

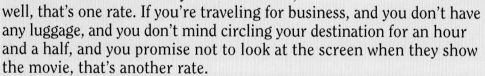

Everything looks so tiny when you're flying. Especially the food they stick in front of you.

How can one ticket on one plane to one place cost a dozen different rates? If you fly between Tuesday and Thursday of concurrent weeks, and you promise to hop down the Jetway on one foot, and you order tickets no less than seven years in advance, well, that's one rate. If you're traveling for business, and you don't have any luggage, and you don't mind circling your destination for an hour and a half, and you promise not to look at the screen when they show the movie, that's another rate.

How badly do any of us want to get anywhere that could make this worth it? Is the fish so fresh in Seattle? Is the sun so warm in Maui? Are the baked beans in Boston really worth it? OK, maybe the beans.

Once you're in the air, it's worse. Now you're the definition of a captive audience, and don't think they don't know it! If your meal or snack (and isn't *that* a thin line?) is cold, hard, late, or eerily floating above your tray table in zero gravity for a second or two, what are you going to do? Ask to see the manager?

I'll let you in on a secret. "Turbulence" is a scam. When that flying tin tube starts rattling, it's just the pilot jostling the joystick to shake loose change out of your pockets.

Get a giant RV, put a tennis ball on the trailer hitch, and make your own destiny. Look for me going 26 mph in the fast lane and shaking my bony fist at planes that pass overhead.

I'm glad the fast-food drive-thru never gets my order right. I don't think my heart could take it.

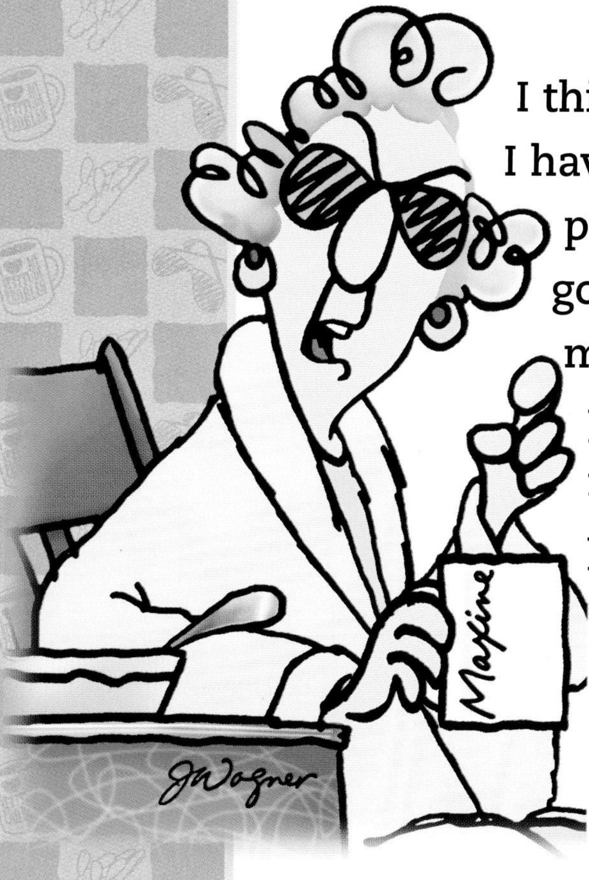
Maxine
JWagner

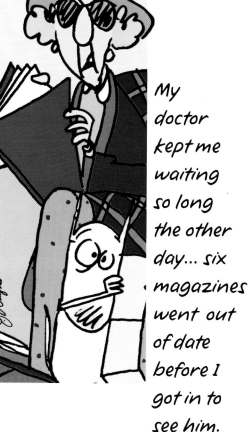

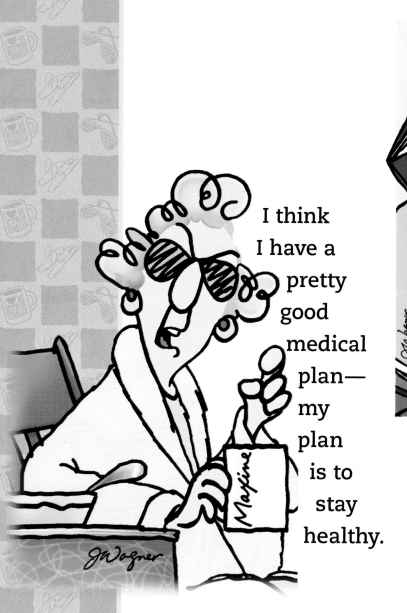

I think I have a pretty good medical plan—my plan is to stay healthy.

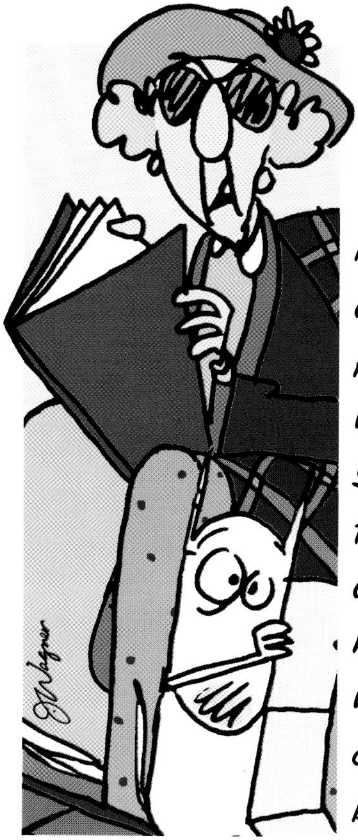
JWagner

My doctor kept me waiting so long the other day... six magazines went out of date before I got in to see him.

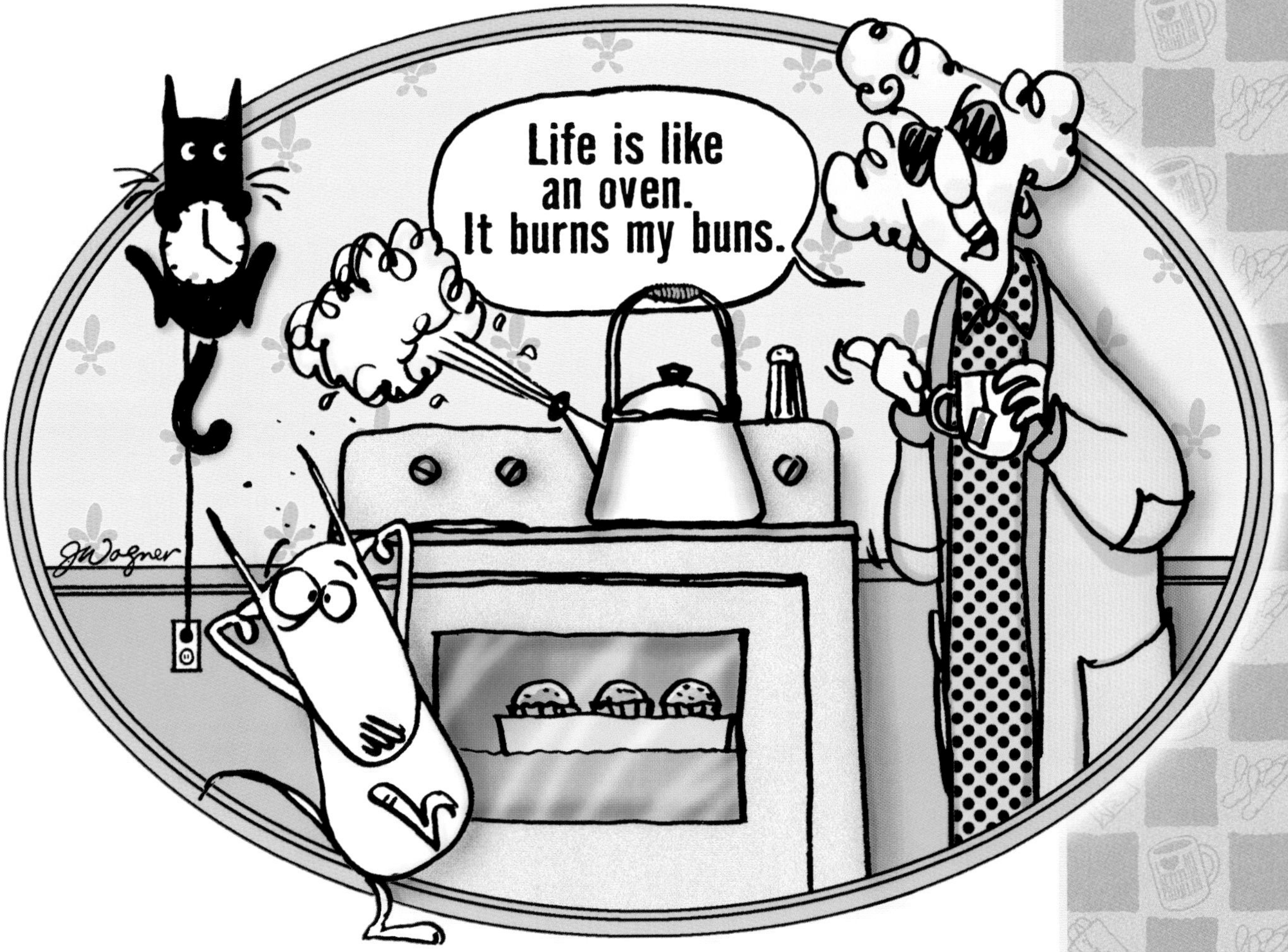
Life is like an oven. It burns my buns.
JWagner

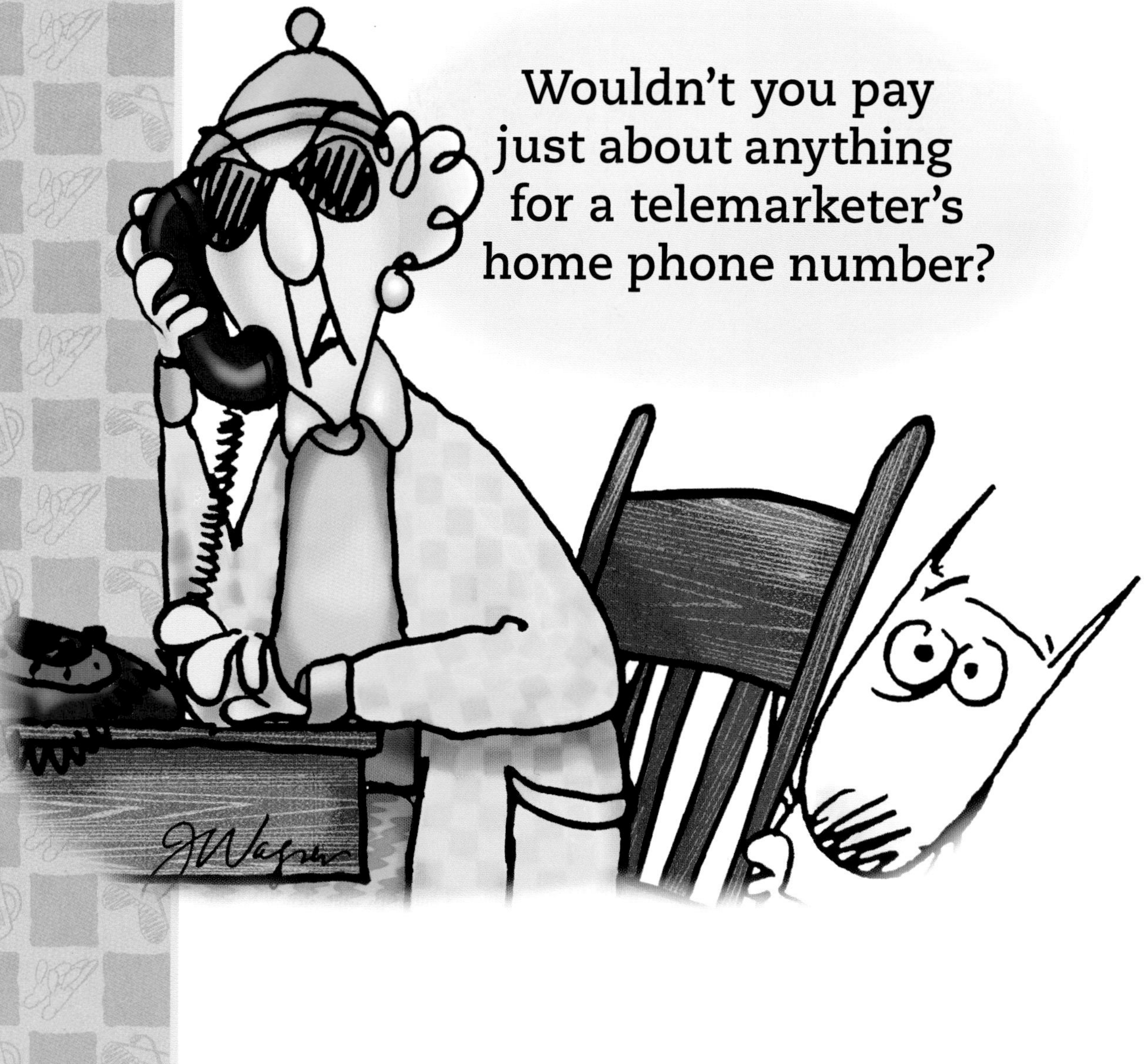
Wouldn't you pay just about anything for a telemarketer's home phone number?

A DAY IN THE STRIFE
A Page From Maxine's Daily Planner

8 a.m. – *Rise and whine. Greet the world with a brisk "Yeah. Whatever."*

8:15 a.m. – *First coffee of the day. First pot of coffee, that is.*

8:30 a.m. – *Need more coffee. I can still separate individual heartbeats.*

9 a.m. – *Three-course breakfast—coffee, cream, and sugar.*

9:30 a.m. – *Make daily list of people I want to offend, annoy, or insult before lunch.*

10 a.m. – *Visit garage sales to look for antiques. But enough about my neighbors.*

11 a.m. – *Organize chores into three categories:*

1. Things I Won't Do Now

2. Things I Won't Do Later

3. Things I'll Never Do

NOON – *Lunch. Go to the "all you can eat" and "all you can regret it later" buffet.*

1:30 p.m. – *Bug the guy in front of me in the eight-item express lane who has ten items, because he's keeping me from going through with my two loaded carts.*

2 p.m. – *Spring cleaning. (In other words, let the dog dust the furniture with his tail.)*

3 p.m. – *Cancel hair appointment; decide that because perms are so expensive, I'll just tie a sleepy blue poodle to my head and get the same effect.*

4 p.m. – *Plant more crabgrass. (Hey, I love the name!)*

5 p.m. – *Wrap garage sale junk to give as wedding gift.*

6 p.m. – *Dinner. Go to drive-thru. Order unhappy meal.*

7 p.m. – *Wedding. Take extra rice. (I love to pelt hard food at happy people.)*

8 p.m. – *Watch a little TV. They repossessed my big TV.*

9 p.m. – *Hit the hay. (Yep. The water balloon just missed the farmer.)*

10 p.m. – *Read a few chapters of HOW TO LOSE FRIENDS AND OFFEND PEOPLE.*

11 p.m. – *Off to la-la land. (And no, I don't mean the relatives' house.)*

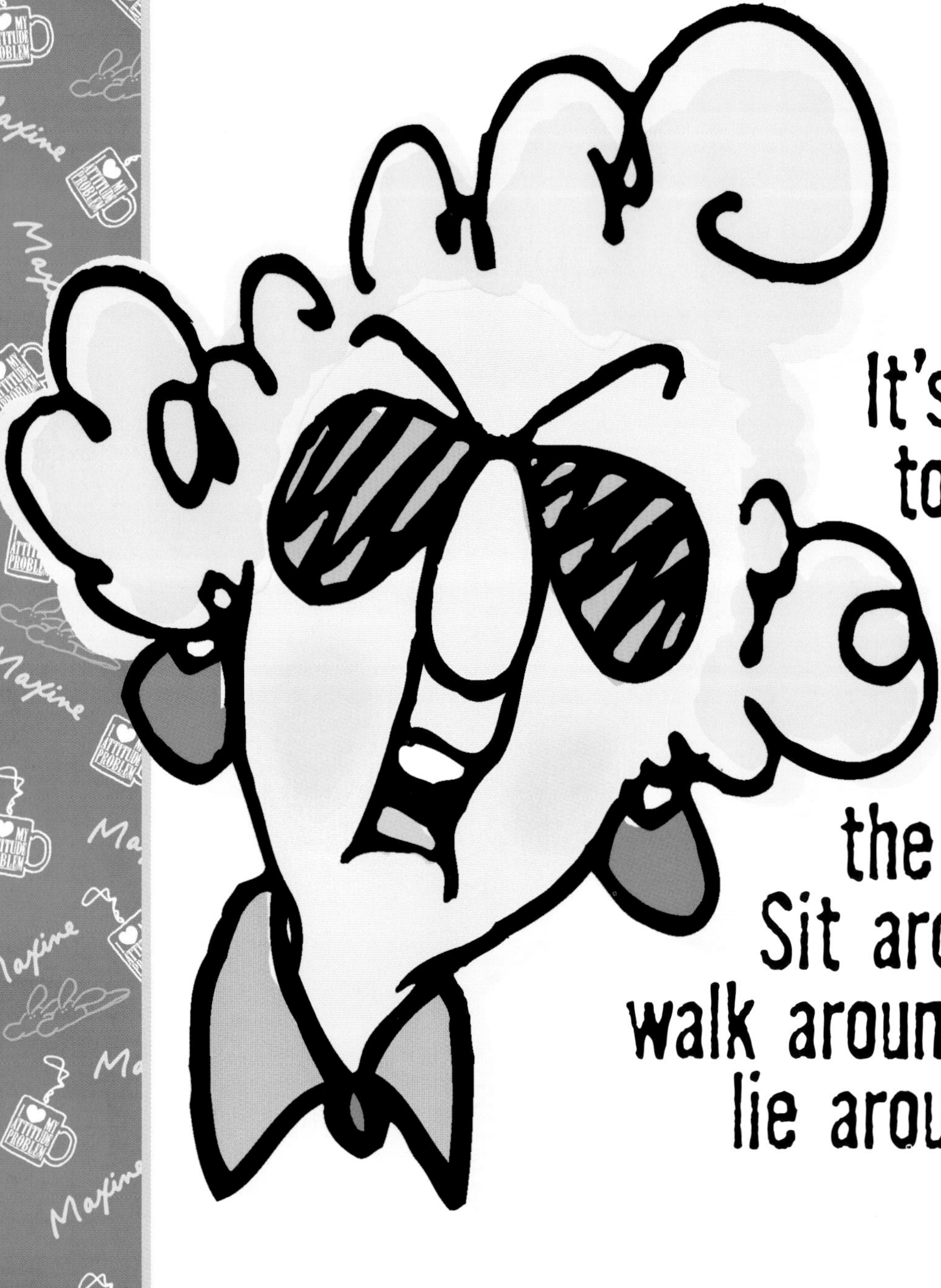

It's time
to do
some
stuff
around
the house.
Sit around it...
walk around it...
lie around it...

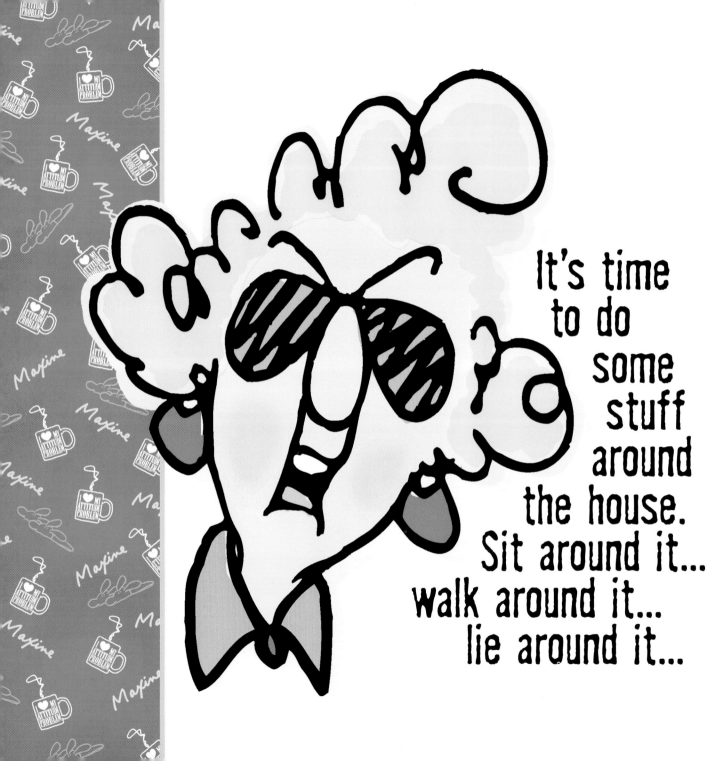

Home Is Where The Heartburn Is

DROP THE KIDS OFF, ADDRESS THE CITY COUNCIL, WHEEL some seniors into the sun, refinish all the woodwork in your house, talk to your mom on the phone, pick the kids up...oh, yeah, and have a challenging, fulfilling, and lucrative career, all the while looking like you just walked out of a catalog ad. Or else you're a failure.

Man, if I cared, the pressure to be perfect would be tighter than bike shorts on a fat aunt. Fortunately, I don't care.

Sometimes there's enough dust on my mantel that I could qualify for federal drought aid. Sometimes my hair looks like I didn't even lather and rinse, much less lather, rinse, and repeat. Sometimes "preparing dinner" means "driving thru." And I guess I could glue little pieces of mirror and colored glass to lots of things and make them character-laden objets d'art, but I've got a nap scheduled. And it looks like it's gonna be a good one.

Wake me when... On second thought, don't wake me. It could be one of those "power naps." And I need all the power I can get.

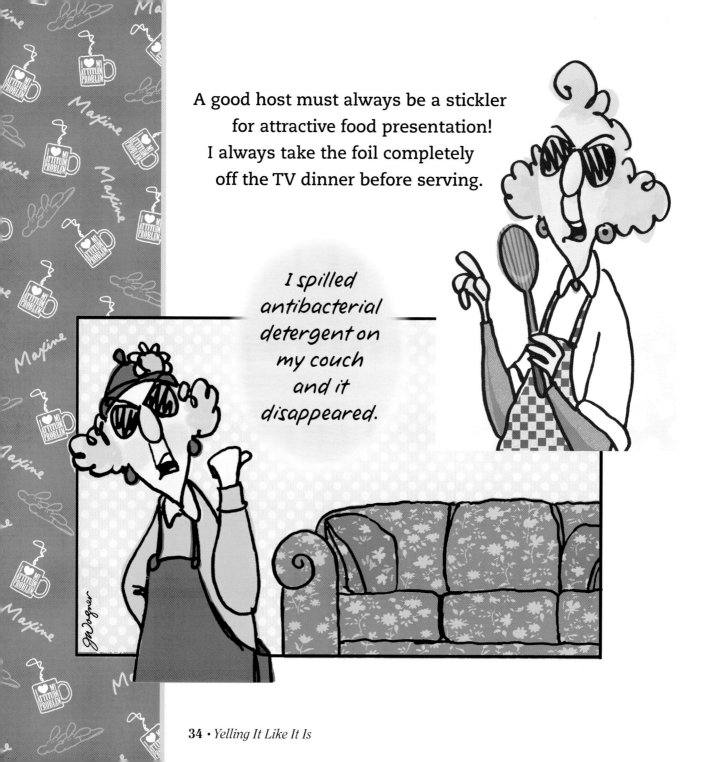

A good host must always be a stickler
for attractive food presentation!
I always take the foil completely
off the TV dinner before serving.

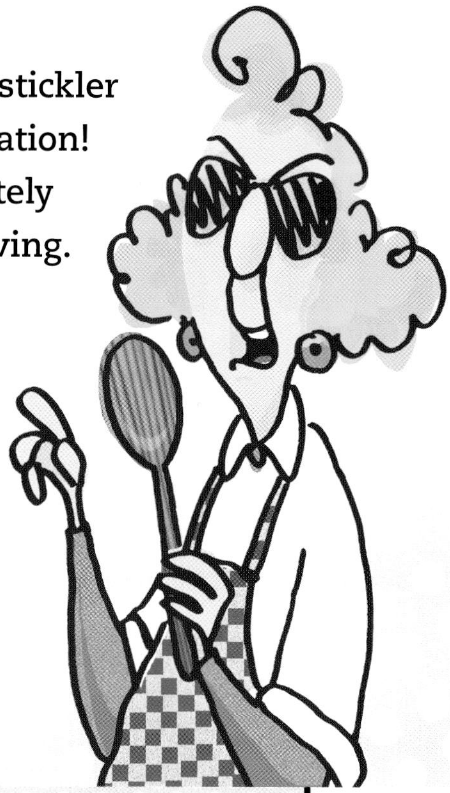

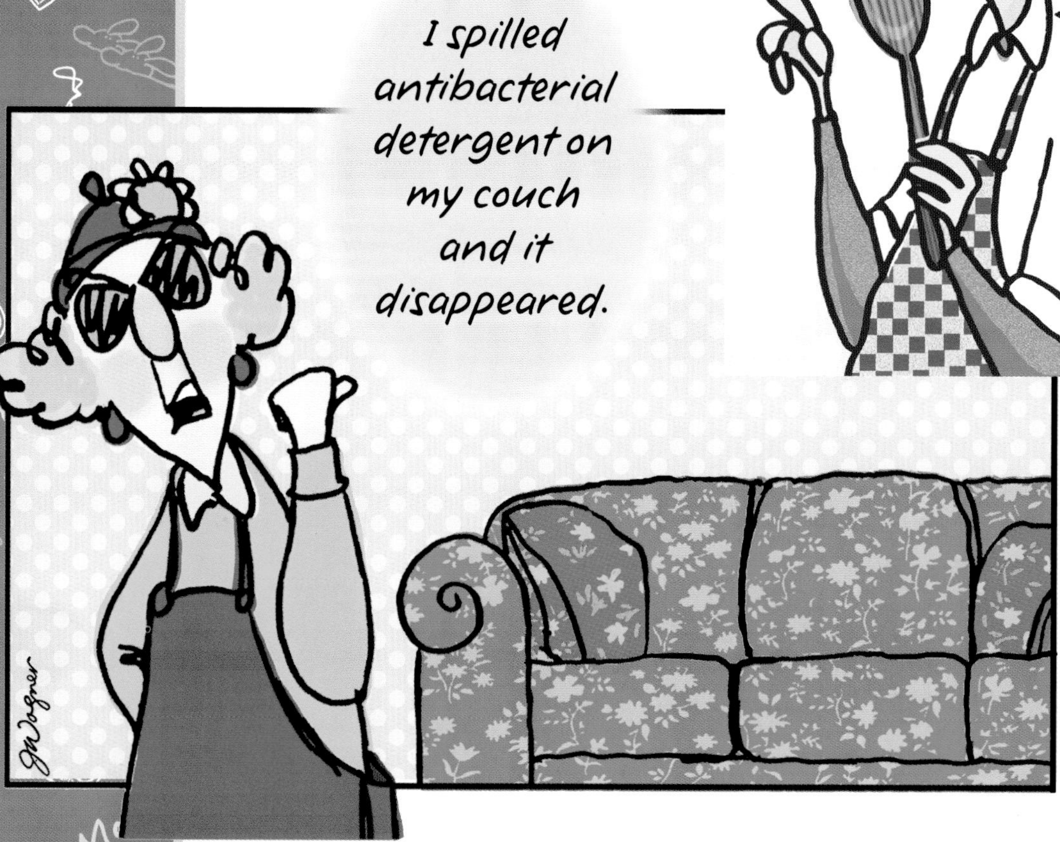
I spilled antibacterial detergent on my couch and it disappeared.

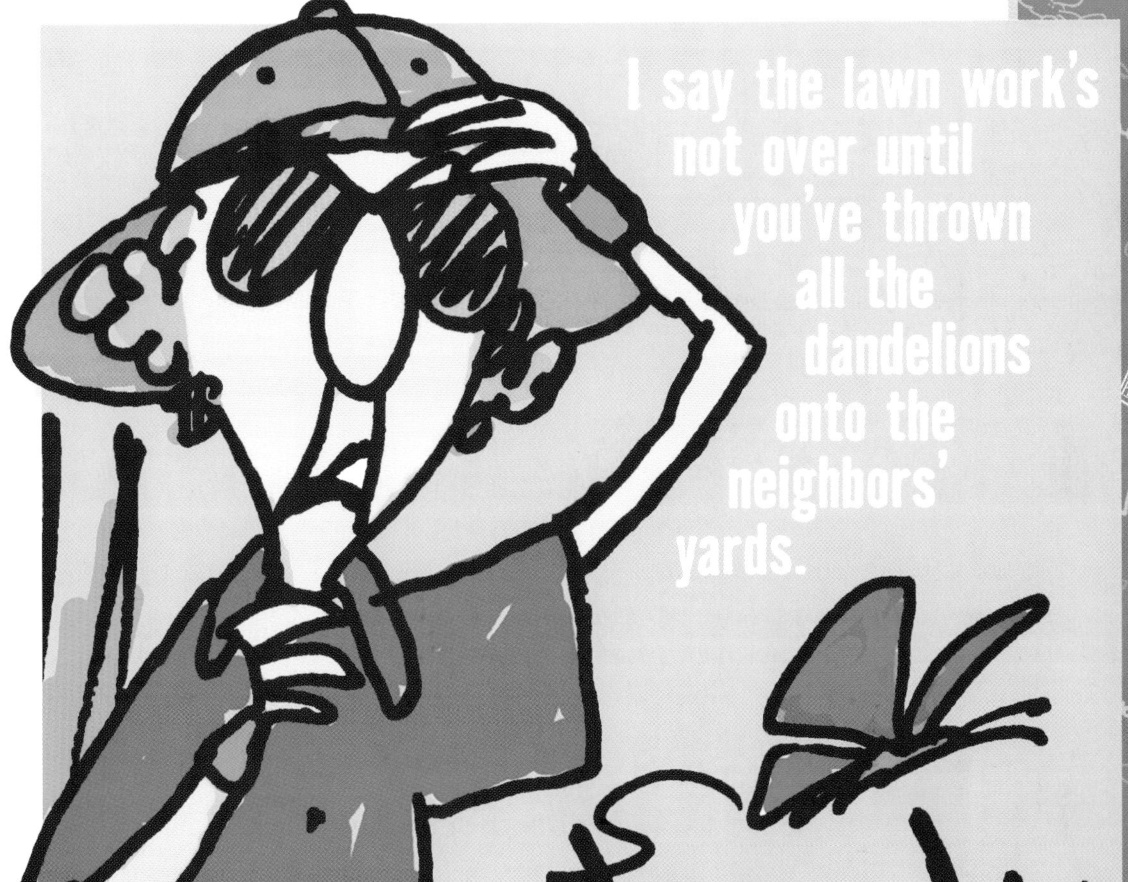
I say the lawn work's not over until you've thrown all the dandelions onto the neighbors' yards.

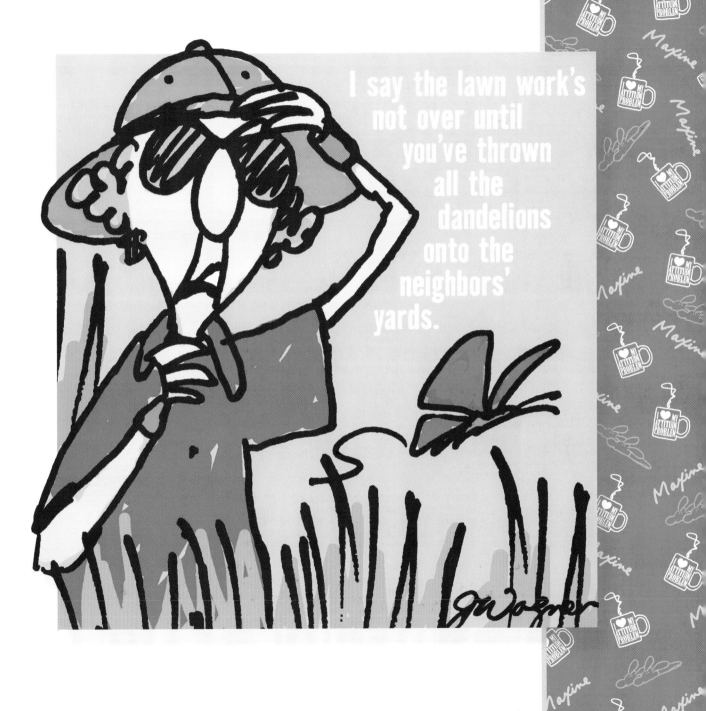

> *Time to think about planting a garden. "Fat chance," I think.*

I DON'T HAVE A GREEN THUMB, but I've got a green finger, if you'd like to see it. OK, it's not green. But bug me about gardening, and you may see it, anyway.

Gardening would be a good idea if not for those big buildings full of food. What do you call them? Oh, yeah, grocery stores. If I grew all my own food, what would become of the self-important teenage managers with their giant rings of keys? When would the checker do her nails or talk to her boyfriend on the phone if not while I stand there glowering? How can my credit card fail to scan if I don't use it?

The only good thing about gardening is the hats. Most people who spend all day pulling weeds are people whose heads are flattered by a really big hat. The bigger, the better. Also, that way you can tell from far off if someone is likely to do the only thing worse than actual gardening, which is *talking about* gardening.

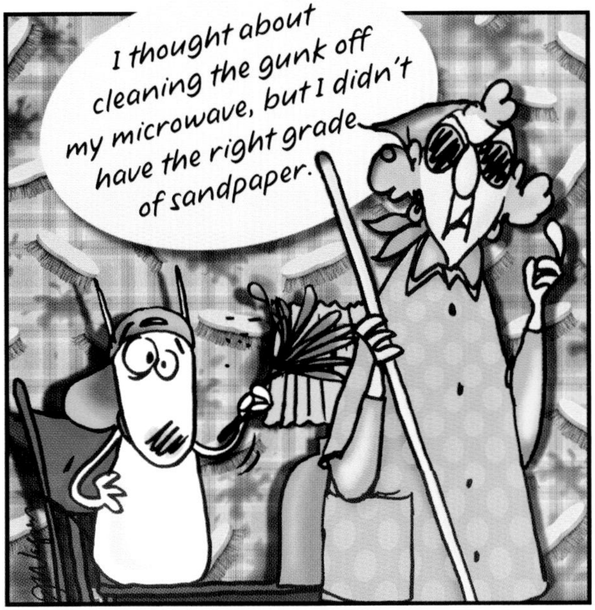
I thought about cleaning the gunk off my microwave, but I didn't have the right grade of sandpaper.

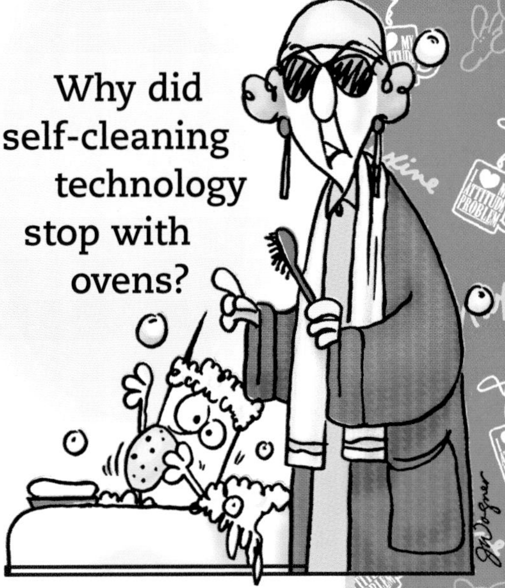

Why did self-cleaning technology stop with ovens?

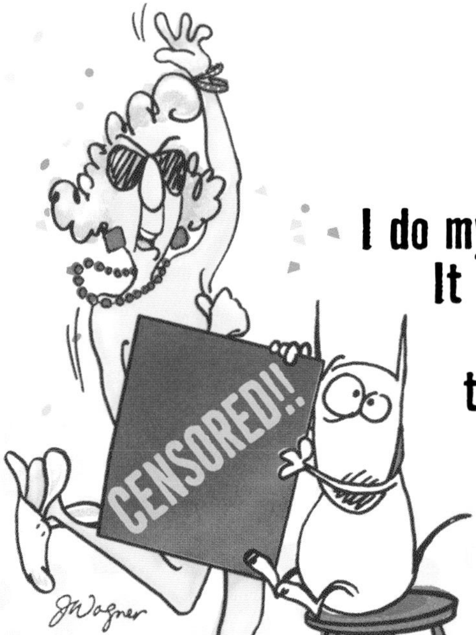
CENSORED!!
JWagner

I do my housework in the nude. It gives me an incentive to clean the mirrors as quickly as possible.

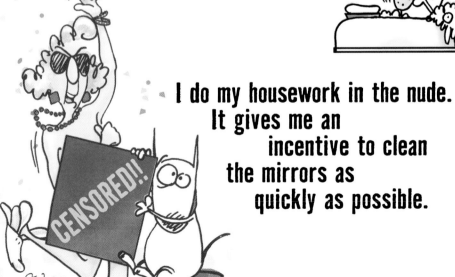

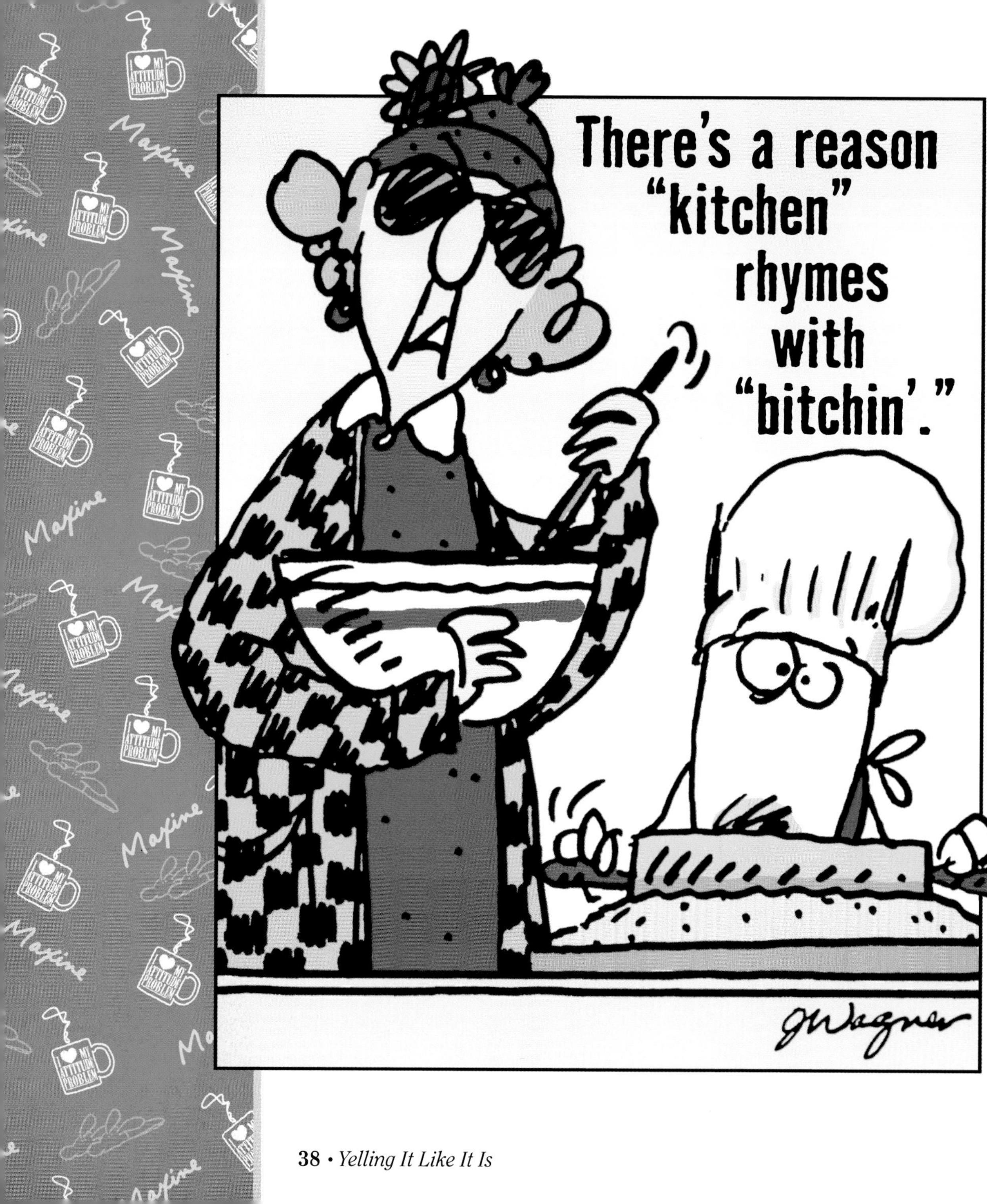
There's a reason "kitchen" rhymes with "bitchin'."
JWagner

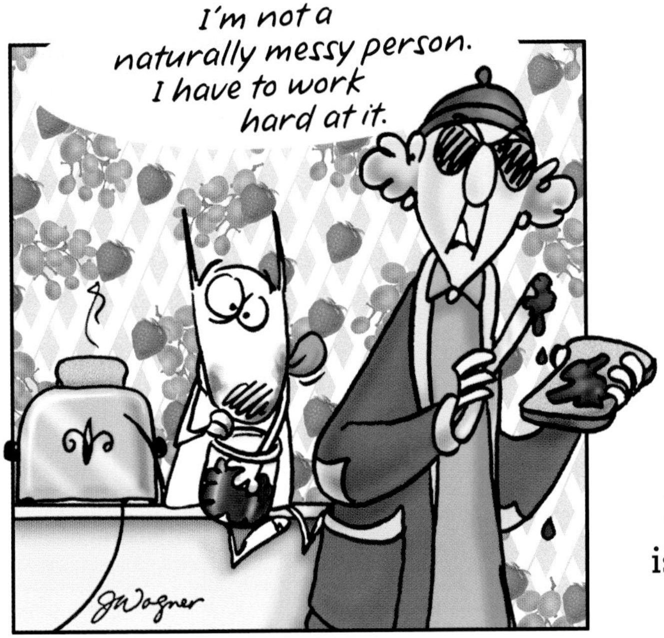
I'm not a naturally messy person. I have to work hard at it.
JWagner

My idea of feng shui is to have them arrange the pepperoni in a circle on my pizza.

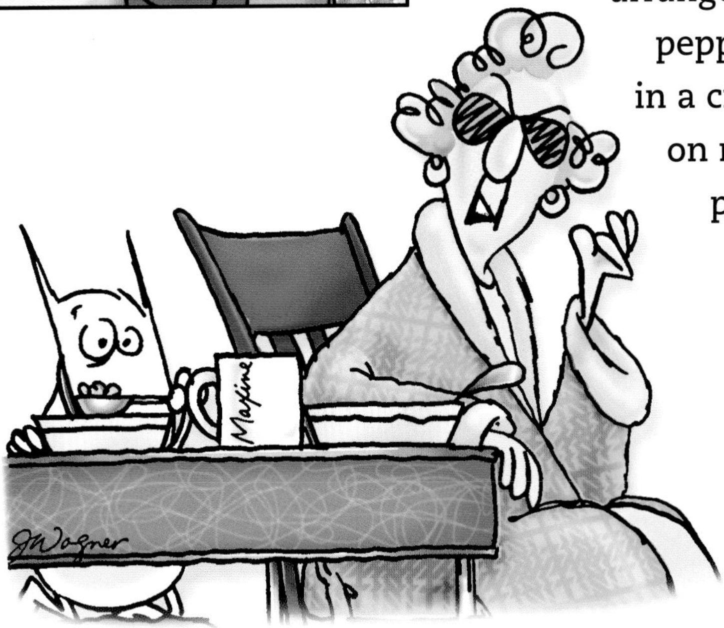
Maxine
JWagner

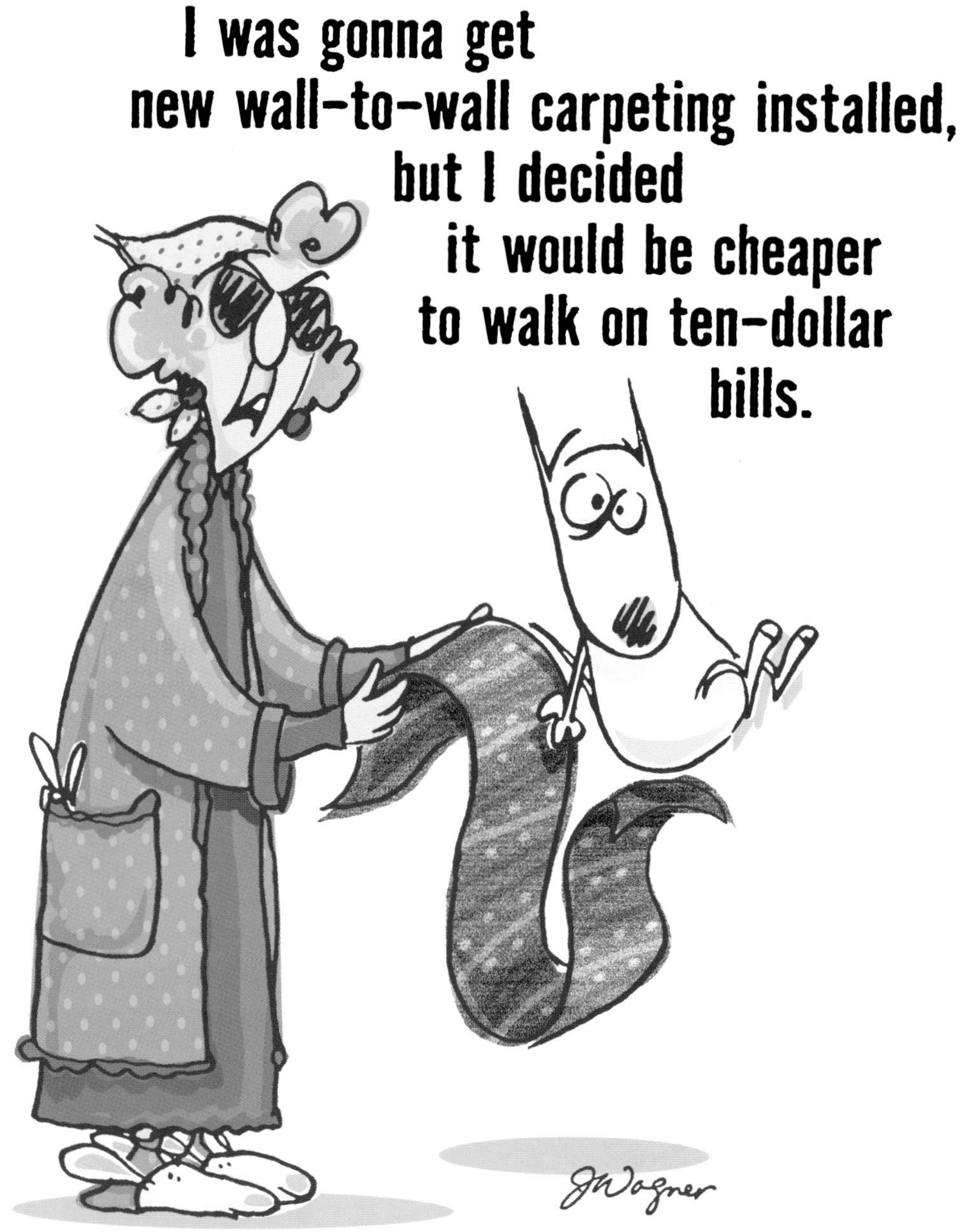
I was gonna get
new wall-to-wall carpeting installed,
but I decided
it would be cheaper
to walk on ten-dollar
bills.

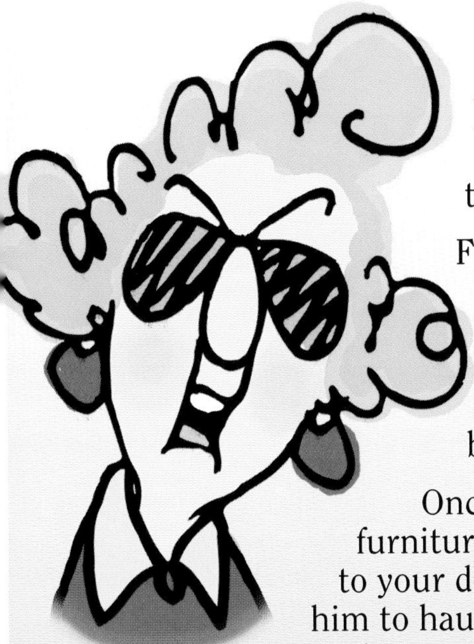

I FINALLY GAVE IN AND GOT MY CARPETS cleaned after receiving 250 coupons in the mail. It's *not* a pleasant experience.

First of all, they only gave me a "range" of time when they'd show up, like "definitely between 6:00 a.m. and 10:30 p.m." Made me want to offer them a range of payments somewhere between "five and ninety-five dollars."

Once they arrived, I had to move all my furniture myself. Until you've lashed a harness to your dog and waved a bone in his face to get him to haul your sectional across the room, you can't say you've had the full experience. On the upside, I found 76 cents, several bobby pins, and a disputed tax return from 1983.

So now these sweaty guys in bib overalls are in my living room dragging wet, noisy machines all over the place and asking if they can use my bathroom.

Finally, they're done, and they tell me to stay off the floors for six to eight hours. Why not just say "seven"?

That's when the staring begins. As their van rattles out of the drive, I'm perched on an island of linoleum surveying the "bad spots" that now show up *more* with what, I've been told, is the result of the deep-cleaning process. They're supposed to disappear as if by magic in six to eight hours. Stopwatch in one hand and cordless phone in the other, my vigil reaches hour seven, minute 59. Then it's 5, 4, 3, 2...speed-dial–REFUND! It's almost more satisfying than actually having clean carpets.

Maxine's Tips for Entertaining

Easy (yet Crabby!) Hints for the Hostess

- When one hosts a dinner party, it is essential that all the place mats match or, at the very least, that they all come from the same fast-food restaurant.

- Entertaining in your backyard? The key to a nice-looking lawn is a good mower. I recommend one who's muscular and shirtless.

- My favorite birthday game is Pin the Cleanup on the Guests.

- Nothing in the world is quite so entertaining as pouring old milk into new containers before having guests over.

- Getting your home in tip-top shape for a party can be fun if you think of it as kicking dust bunny butt!

- Take shortcuts! I used to offer my guests instant coffee. They kept whining for hot water to go with it.

- The best way to prepare a roast is to make an aluminum foil tent over your roasting pan. Similarly, the best way to prepare for relatives is to pitch a tent in the backyard and stay there until they leave.

- When decorating for a party, be creative with regular household items. Some people might just see a moldy shower curtain with torn eyelets. What do I see? A new tablecloth.

- The better you cook, the more likely your guests will return. Which is why I'm usually not too hot in the kitchen.

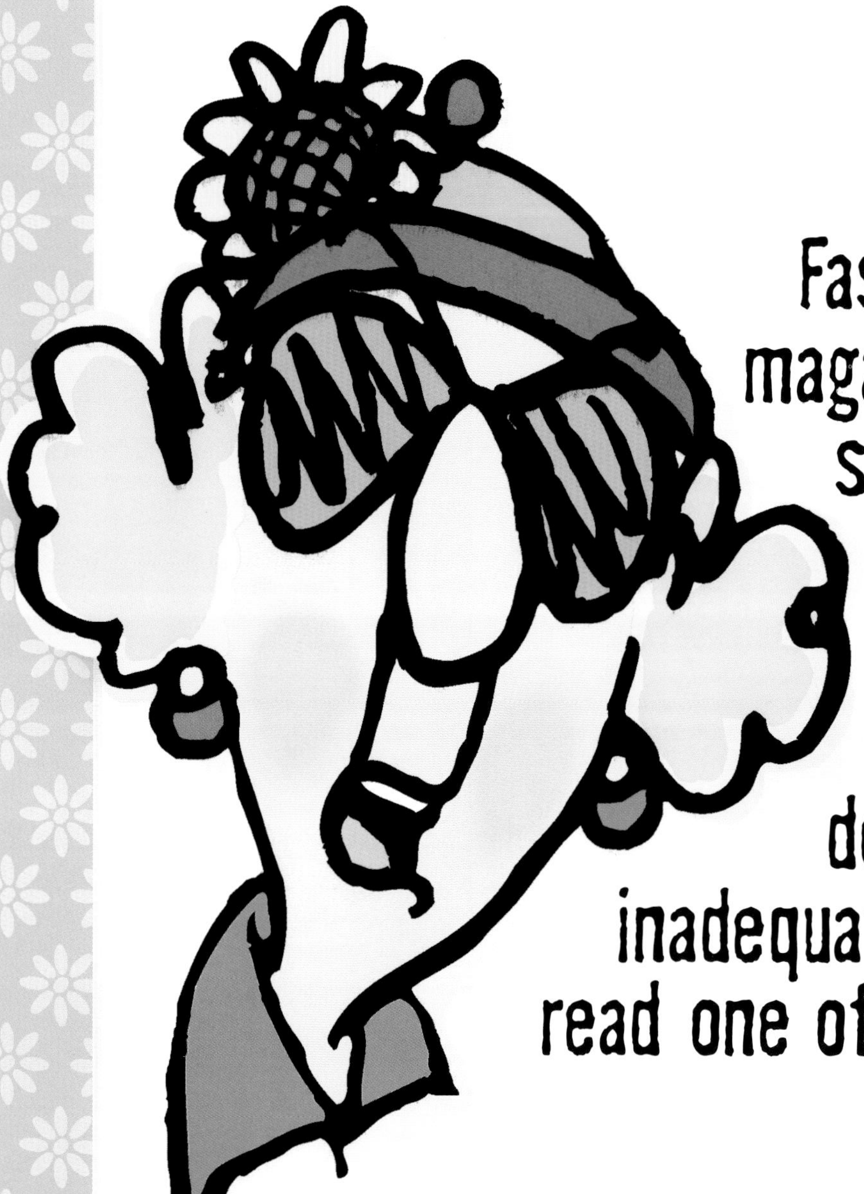

Fashion magazines are society's way of saying "If you don't feel inadequate already, read one of these!"

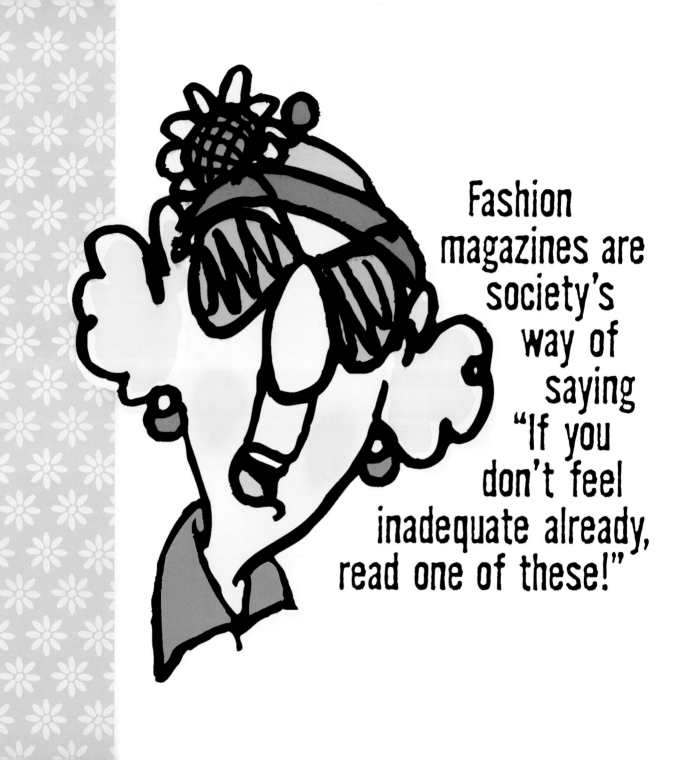

Fashionably Crabby

Want to lose 20 pounds before swimsuit season while eating whatever you want? Learn how to make your man read you poetry? Turn your high school classmates green with envy at your class reunion? If you've got about $5.95, there's a magazine that can do it. Or so they scream from racks in every grocery store, gas station, and airport souvenir shop.

Women's magazines show pictures of enhanced, starved supermodels airbrushed into some photo editor's idea of perfection. Then they tell you how you can achieve the look without leaving your house. Of course, if their tips worked, you'd never have to buy another magazine. Ever.

Here's another thing. The "better" the magazine, the more ad pages it sells. This is like saying the better the TV show, the more commercials it runs.

You *can* lose 20 pounds quickly with this easy system–grab four magazines and throw them away. Repeat as necessary.

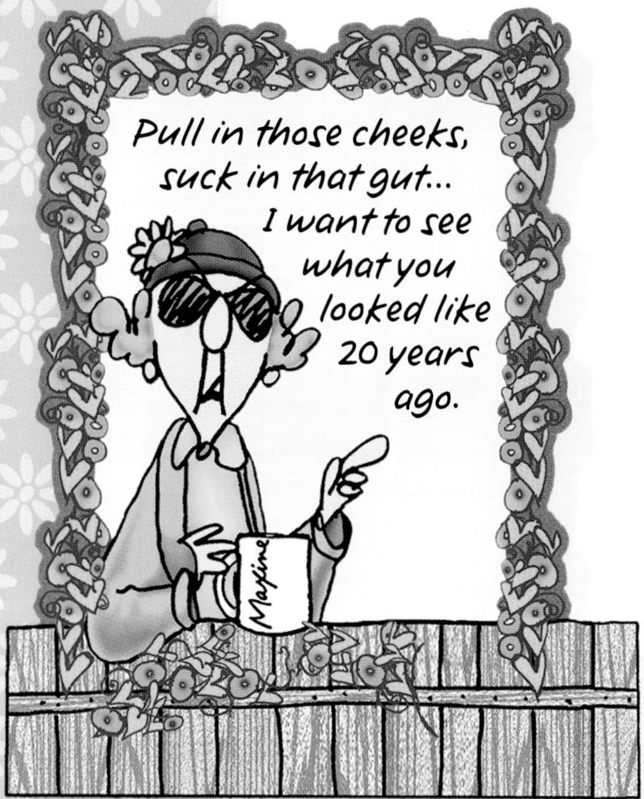
Pull in those cheeks,
suck in that gut...
I want to see
what you
looked like
20 years
ago.
Maxine

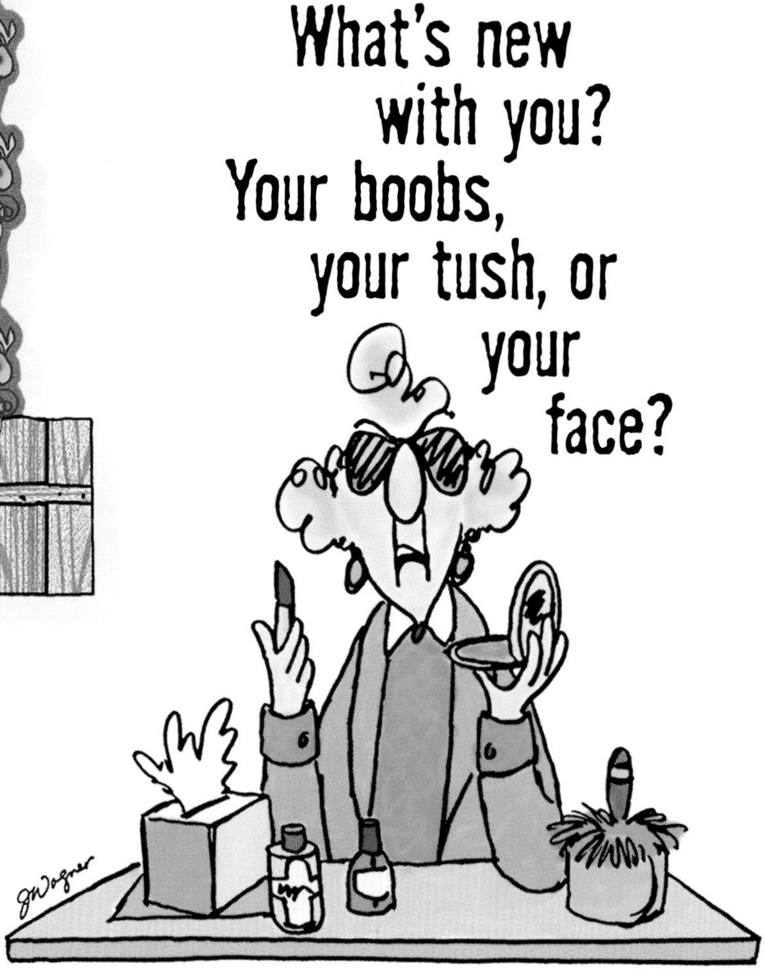
What's new
with you?
Your boobs,
your tush, or
your
face?
JWagner

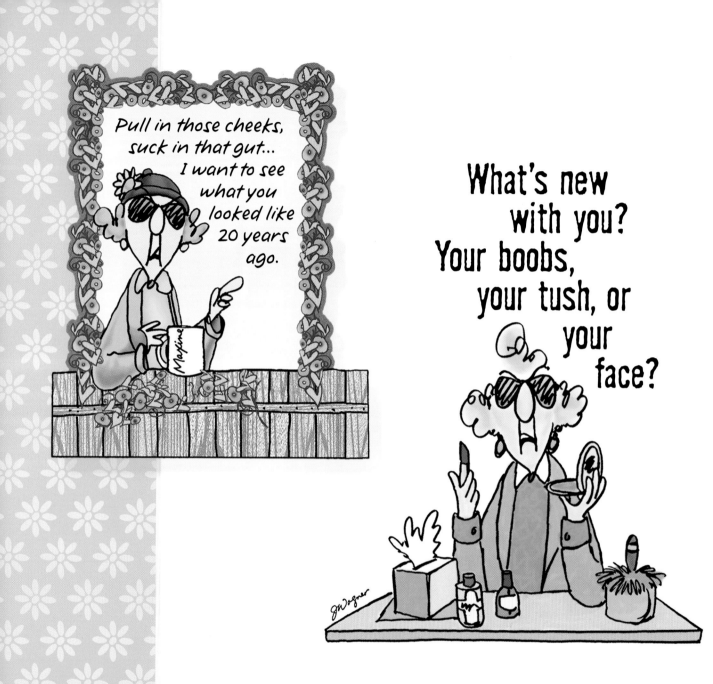

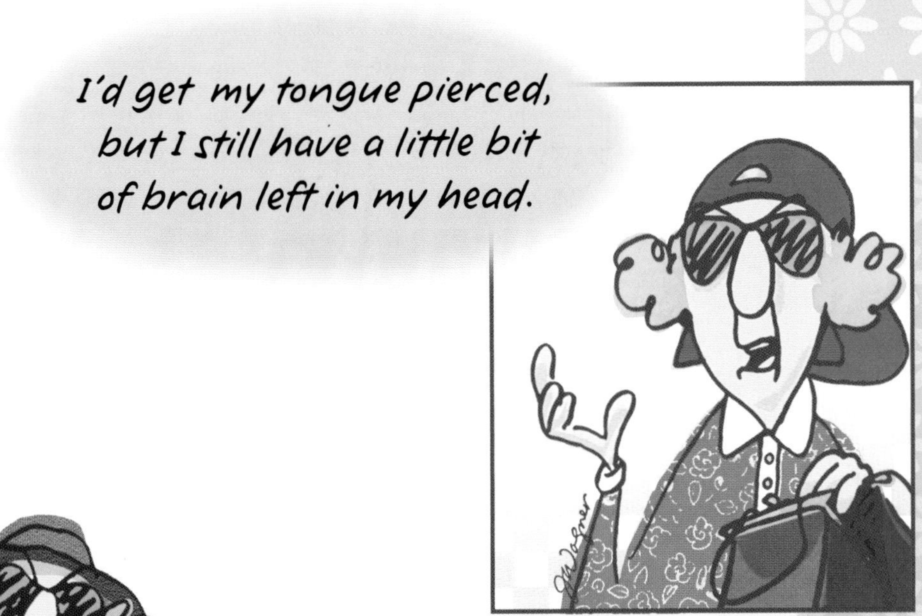
I'd get my tongue pierced, but I still have a little bit of brain left in my head.

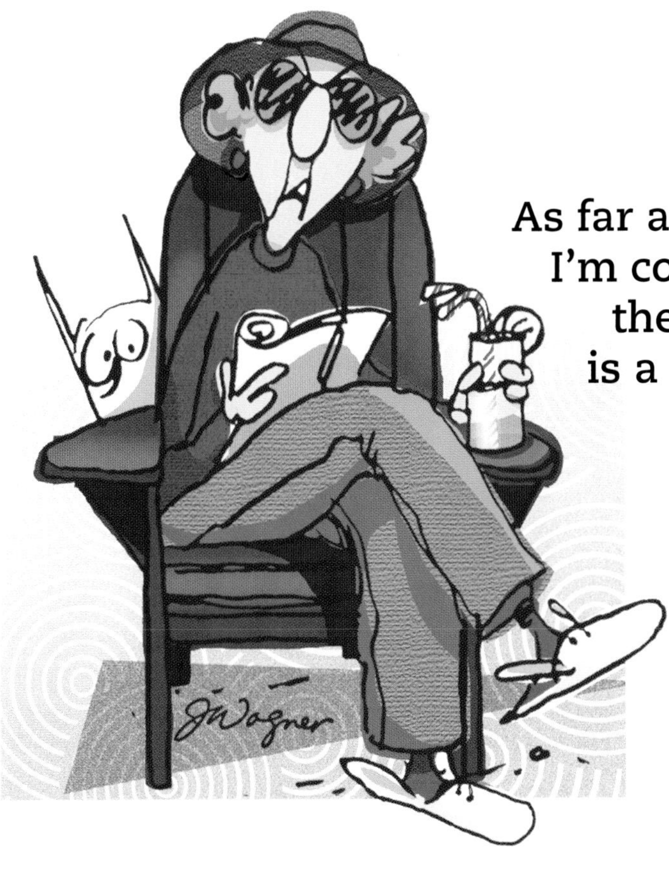

As far as
I'm concerned,
the perfect bra
is a sweatshirt.

When I see a sign that says "All sales are final," I take that as a personal challenge.

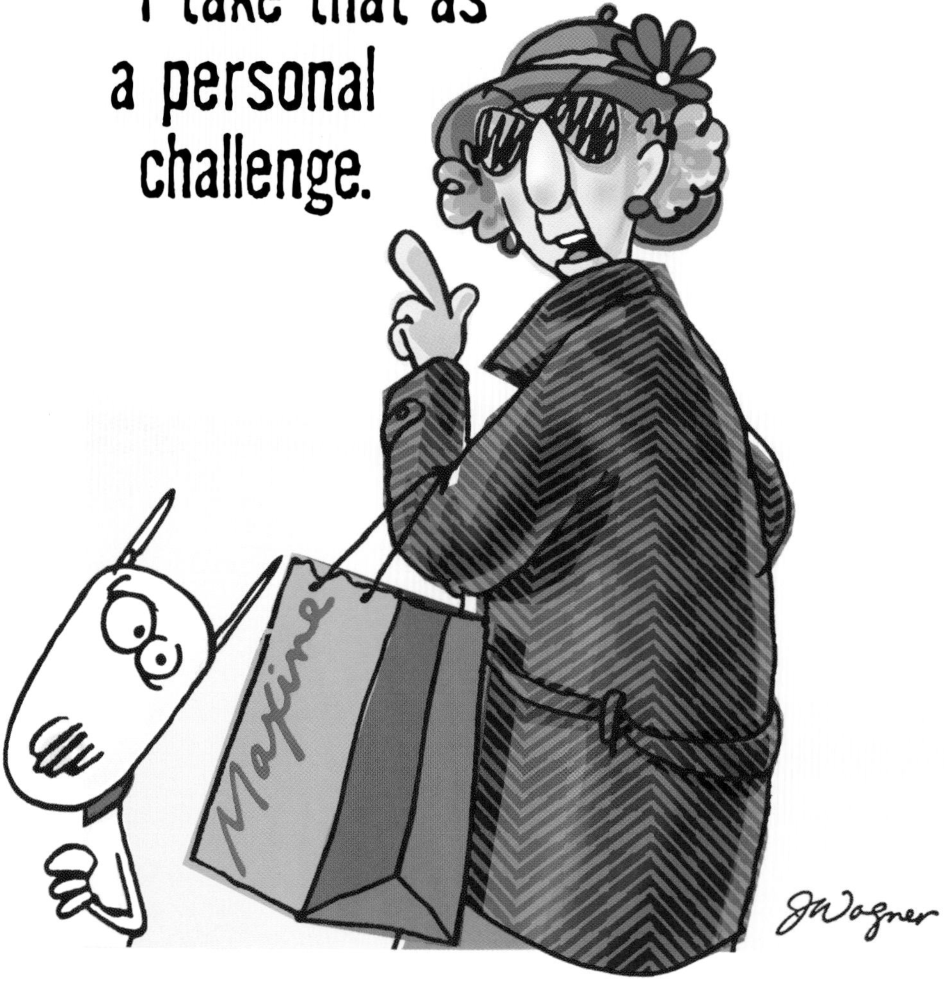
Maxine
JWagner

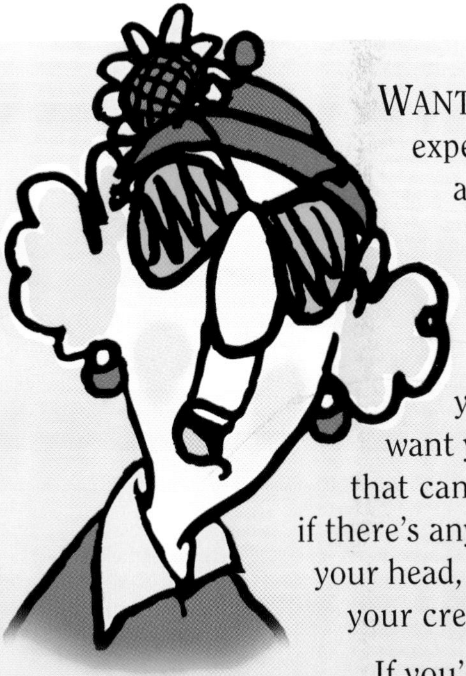

WANT TO HAVE A DEHUMANIZING experience that will cost you not only all your money but also most of your self-esteem? Visit a boutique. They're called "boo-tiques" because the prices jump out and scare you. Boutiques hire women who hate you, who hold you in contempt, who want you to sense a vacuum in your closet that can only be filled by them. Of course, if there's any item of clothing you can pull over your head, jam your legs into, or squeeze onto your credit card, it's *you*!

If you're lucky, the boutique will be busy and you'll just get the "let me know if I can help" nod from the salesperson. This is your chance to grab some clothes from the sale table (where prices have been reduced from Ridiculous to merely Outlandish) and try them on without the hovering clerk. Thus, you're rescued from the disapproving looks that silently say, "Careful–that fabric can only stretch so far" and "Frankly, that blouse color clashes with your ugly shoes."

It's a good idea to shop in teams. If one of you falls for a slippery sale, the other can pull you out by the purse strap. Plus, a friend can help in the post-shopping snacking. She can order the dessert you thought you might want instead of the dessert you did order. Then you can share.

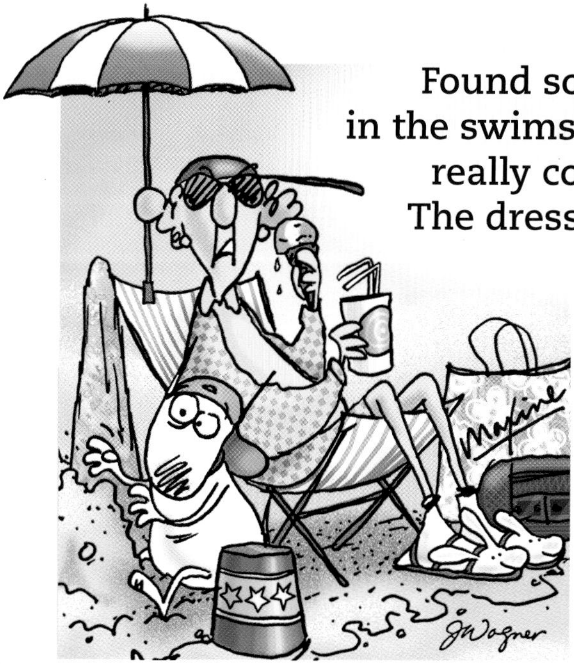
Maxine
JWagner

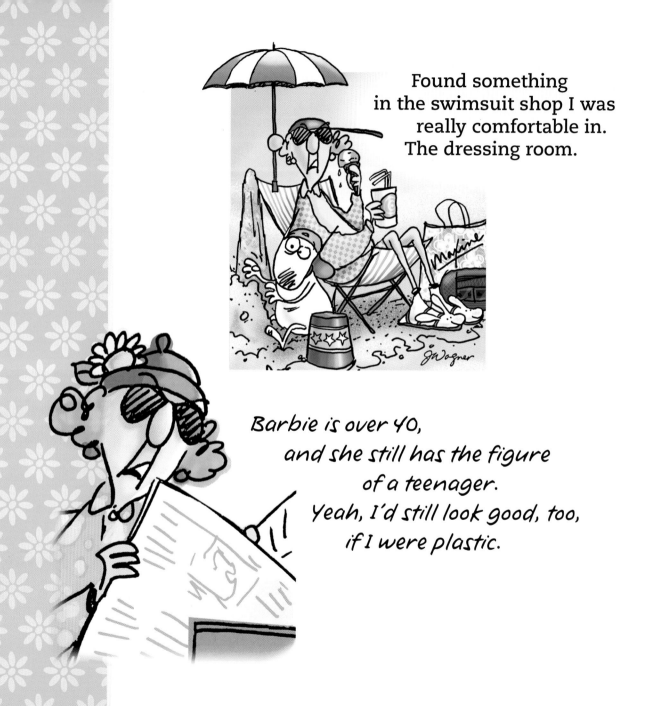

Found something
in the swimsuit shop I was
really comfortable in.
The dressing room.

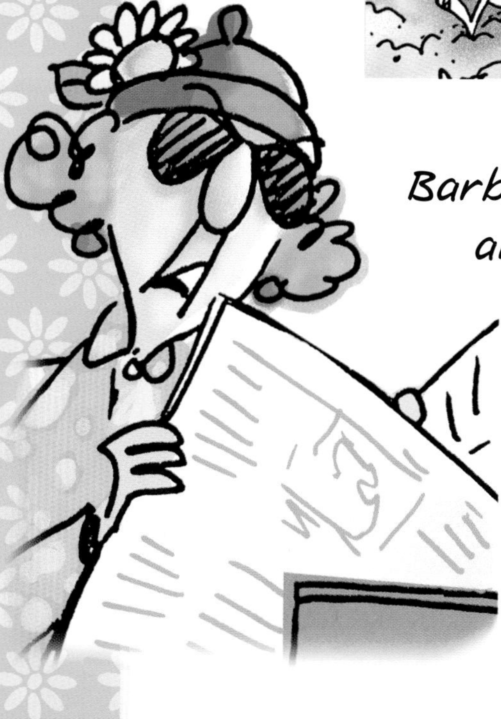

*Barbie is over 40,
and she still has the figure
of a teenager.
Yeah, I'd still look good, too,
if I were plastic.*

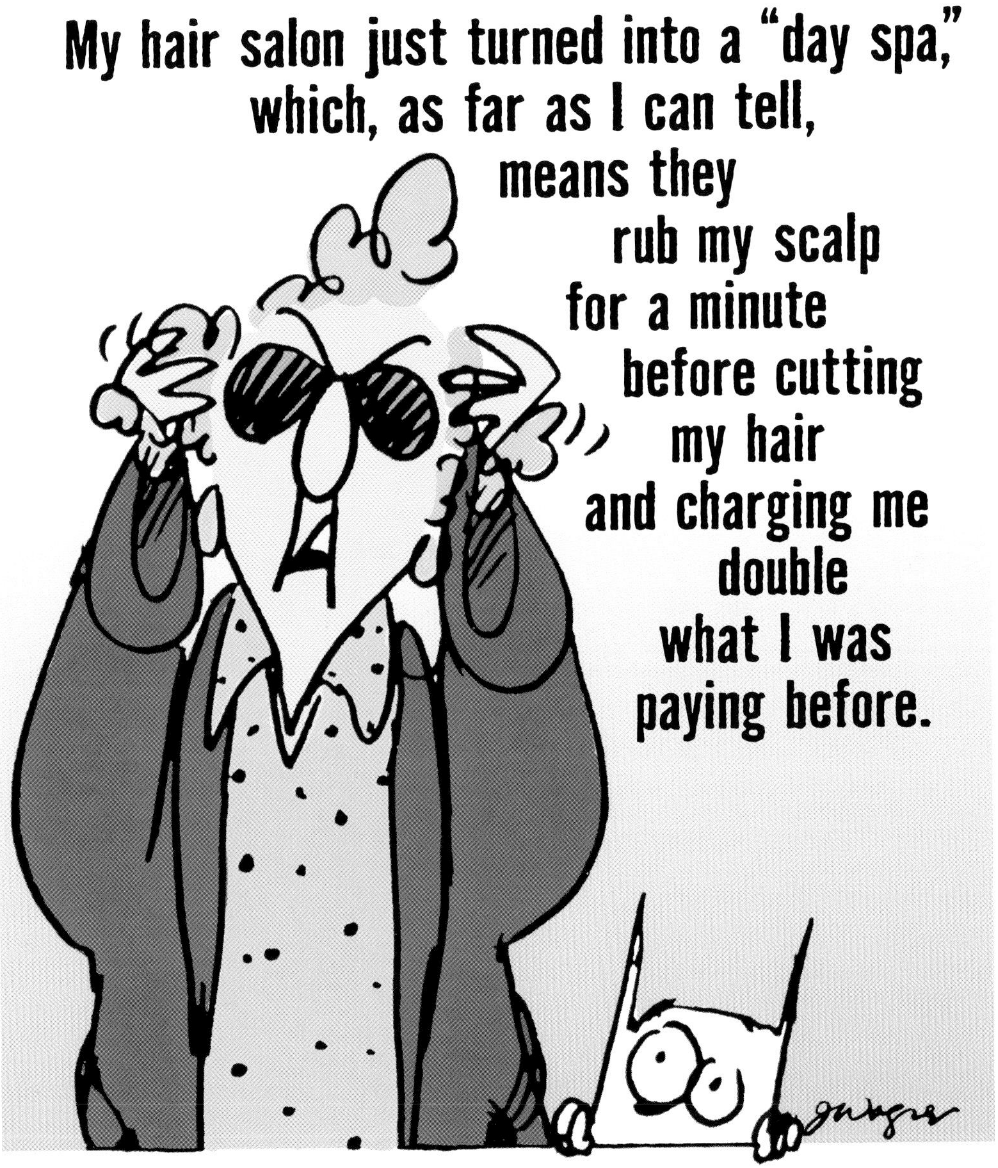
My hair salon just turned into a "day spa," which, as far as I can tell, means they rub my scalp for a minute before cutting my hair and charging me double what I was paying before.

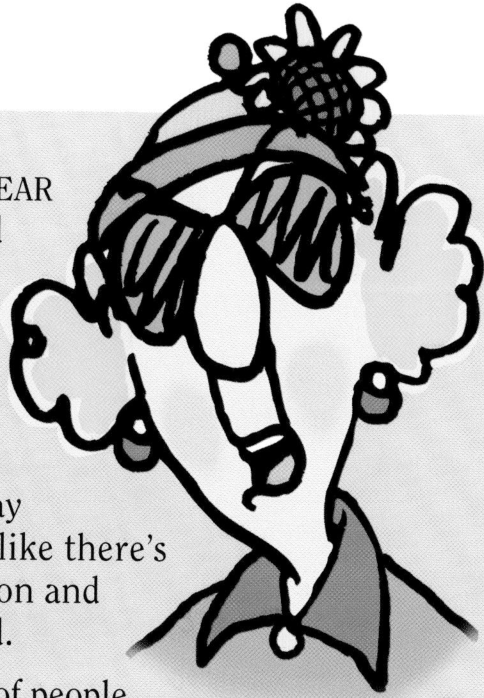

MANY PEOPLE MY AGE WEAR wigs. They seem fake and obvious and more than a little sad. And the ones on the women are just as bad.

I've got to admit that I fluctuate between the gray and the blue. It's kind of like there's a civil war of tints going on and my scalp is the battlefield.

On vacation, I saw lots of people getting beads braided into their hair. I considered it until I realized that my clacking head would make it impossible to sneak over to the neighbor's yard to grab his paper.

I remember when a haircut cost a nickel. Not really, but $55 plus a tip seems like a lot to get my ends trimmed. I'm never sure about tipping either. I read somewhere that hairstylists consider themselves professionals and tips insult them. Or maybe I made that up myself. Either way, it sounds dead-on to me.

For $90, a permanent really should be, you know, permanent.

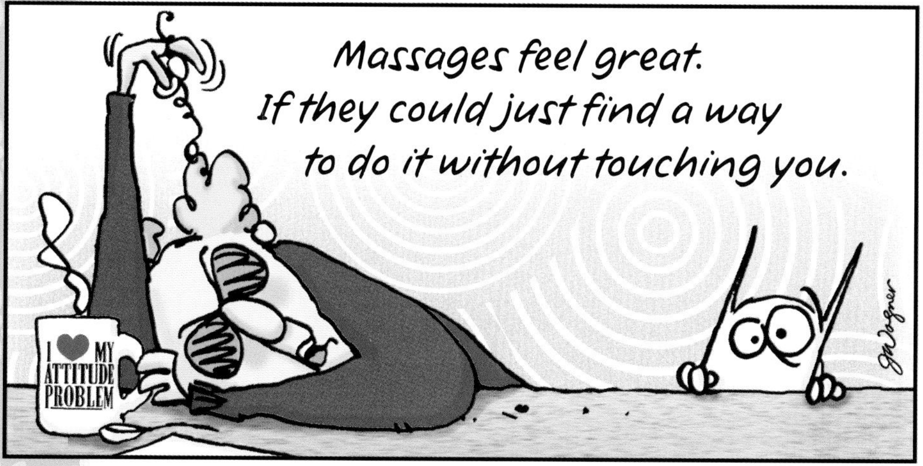
Massages feel great.
If they could just find a way
to do it without touching you.
I ♥ MY ATTITUDE PROBLEM

**Ah, the thrill of
watching kicking,
blocking, tackling,
running...
but enough
about fall sales
at the mall.**

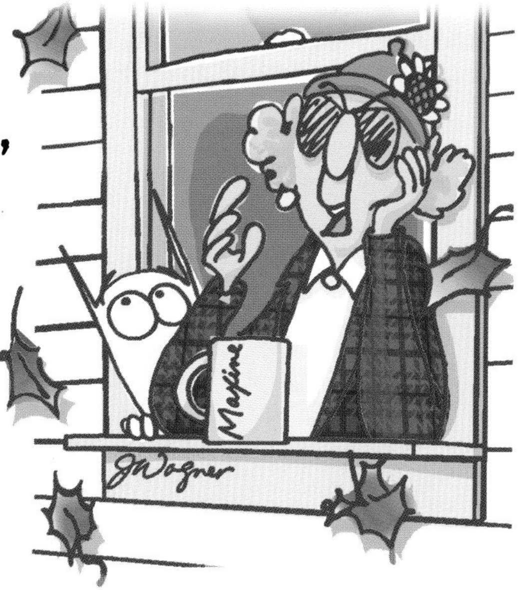
Maxine

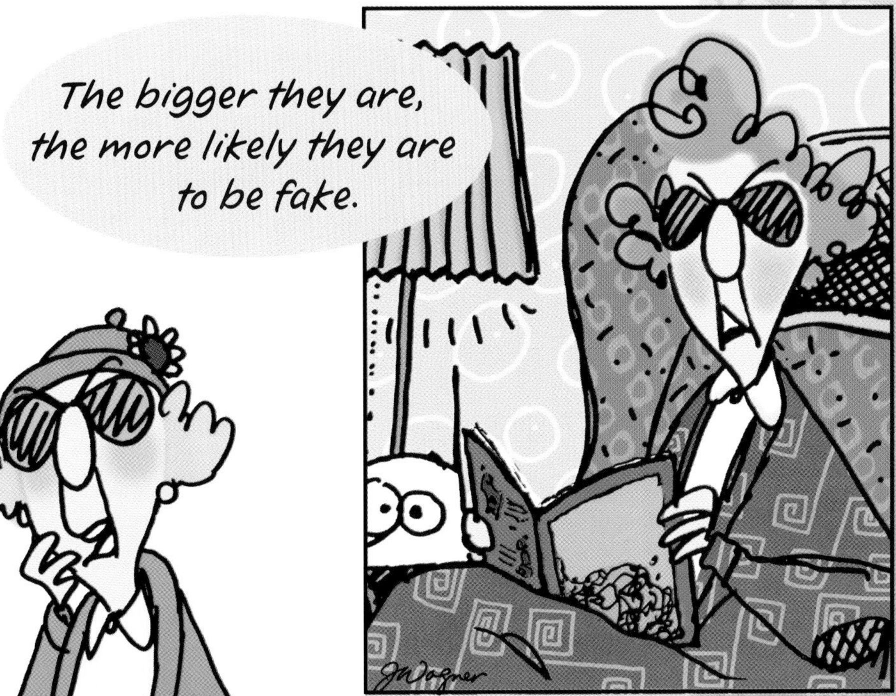
The bigger they are, the more likely they are to be fake.

I'd get
a tattoo
if I had
any skin
tight
enough
to draw
on.

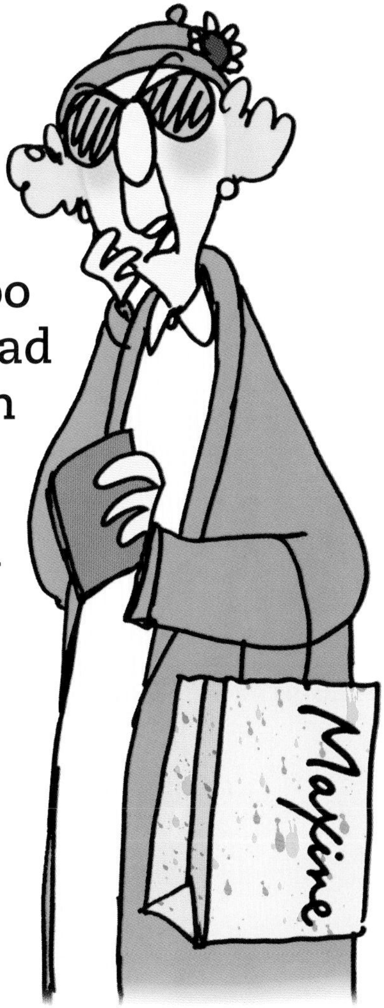
Maxine

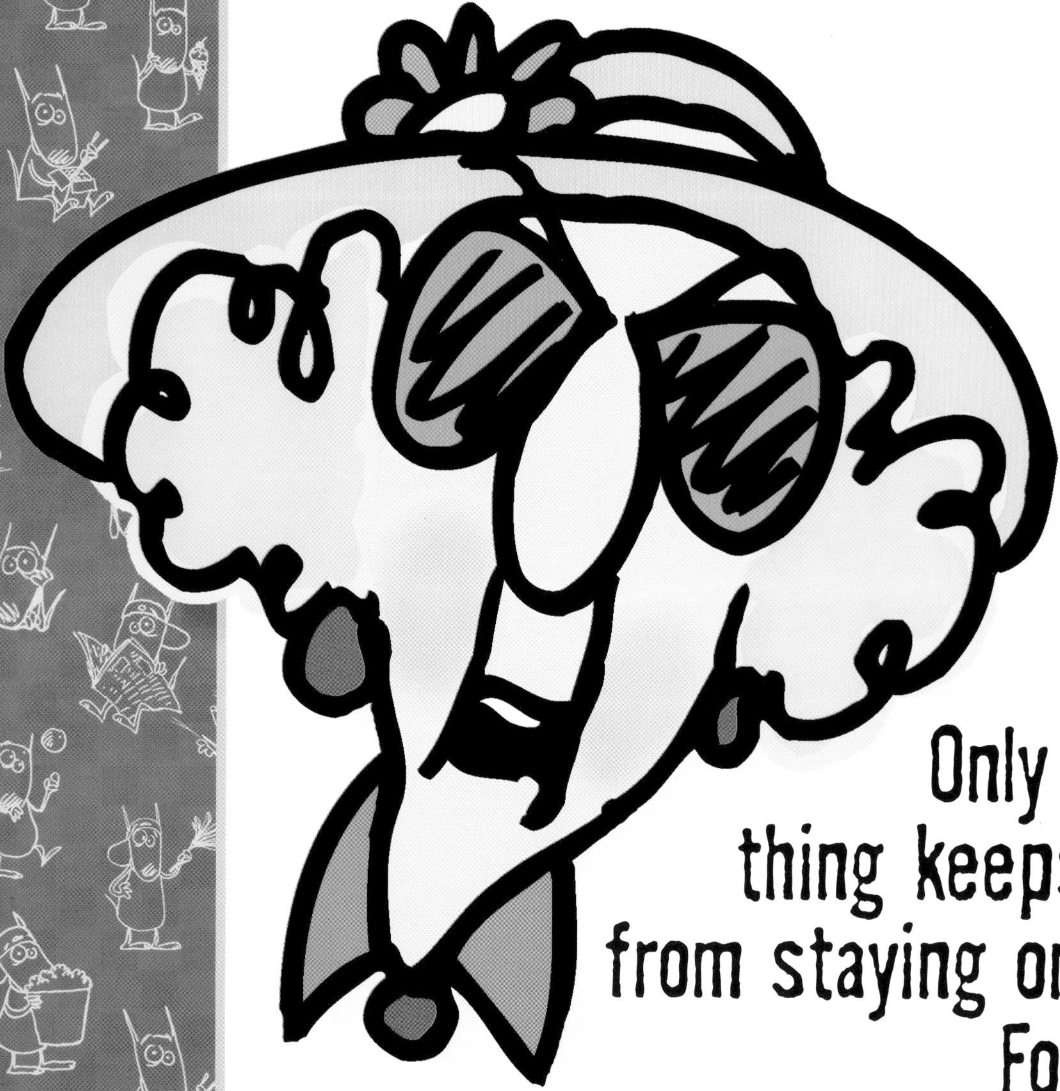

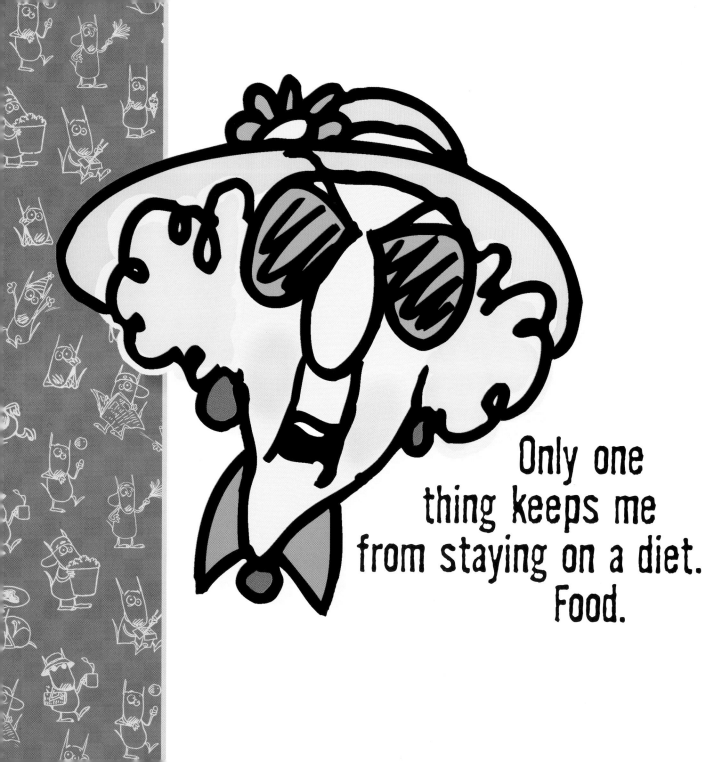

Only one
thing keeps me
from staying on a diet.
Food.

Shape Up Or Chip Out

AFTER LOOKING THROUGH AS MANY MAGAZINES AS I COULD before they threatened to kick me out of the bookstore, I was able to determine what the "experts" consider the perfect diet for someone of my age, height, ward, precinct, and trash-pickup day:

Breakfast: Unbuttered toast, orange rind, 1/4 cup of decaf coffee, and one fried egg (smelled, not eaten).

Lunch: 3 medium-length celery stalks, lick the lid of a skim milk bottle, and a raisin. Then for dessert... Oh, wait, the raisin was dessert.

Supper: Any combination of the above plus fat-free, soy-based, plain yogurt with a cherry on top (cherry for decoration only).

If I actually ate what I'm supposed to, I'd lose weight, because I'd never feel like eating. Do the weight-loss wackos who come up with these diets actually try them?!

The only fad diet that's made sense to me is the protein-based diet. At least you get meat. Lots and lots of meat. Meat trucks pull up to your door. Birds of prey circle your garbage disposal. After three weeks on that diet, you begin to pack a club and look for mastodons.

I have to take
so many
vitamin supplements now
that I'm too full
to eat any actual food.

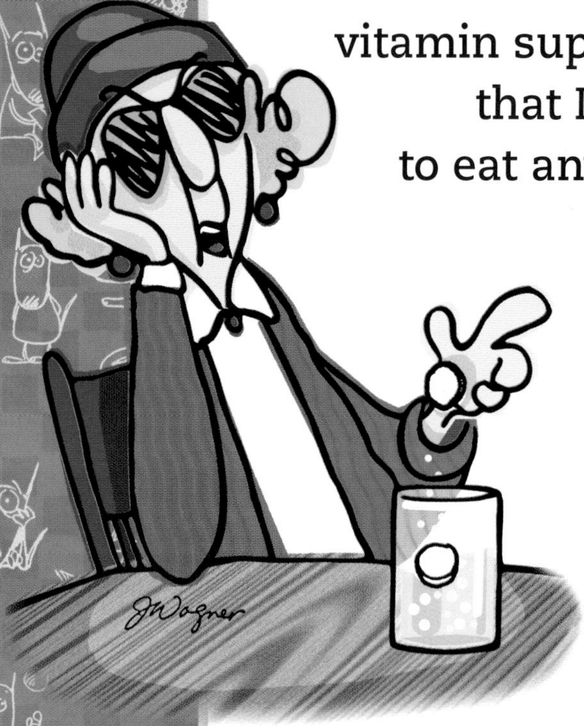

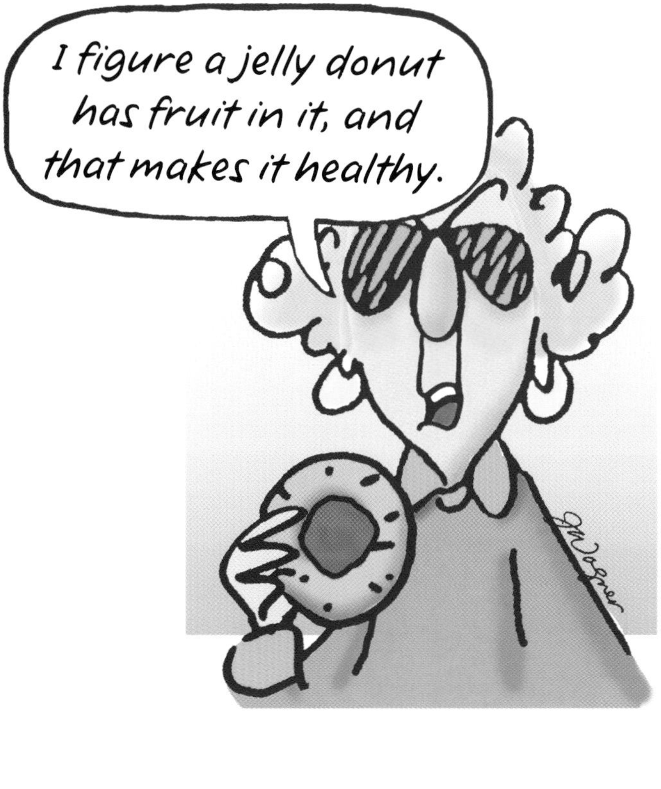
I figure a jelly donut has fruit in it, and that makes it healthy.

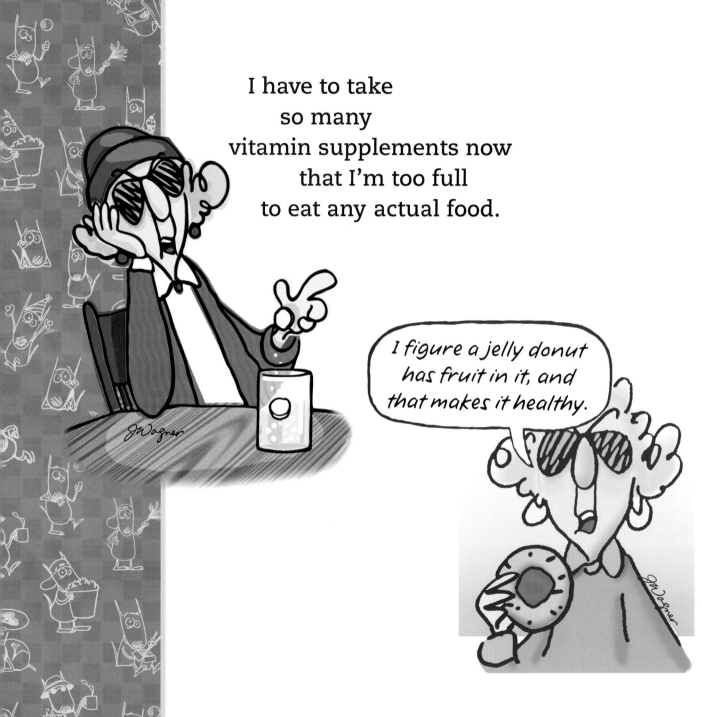

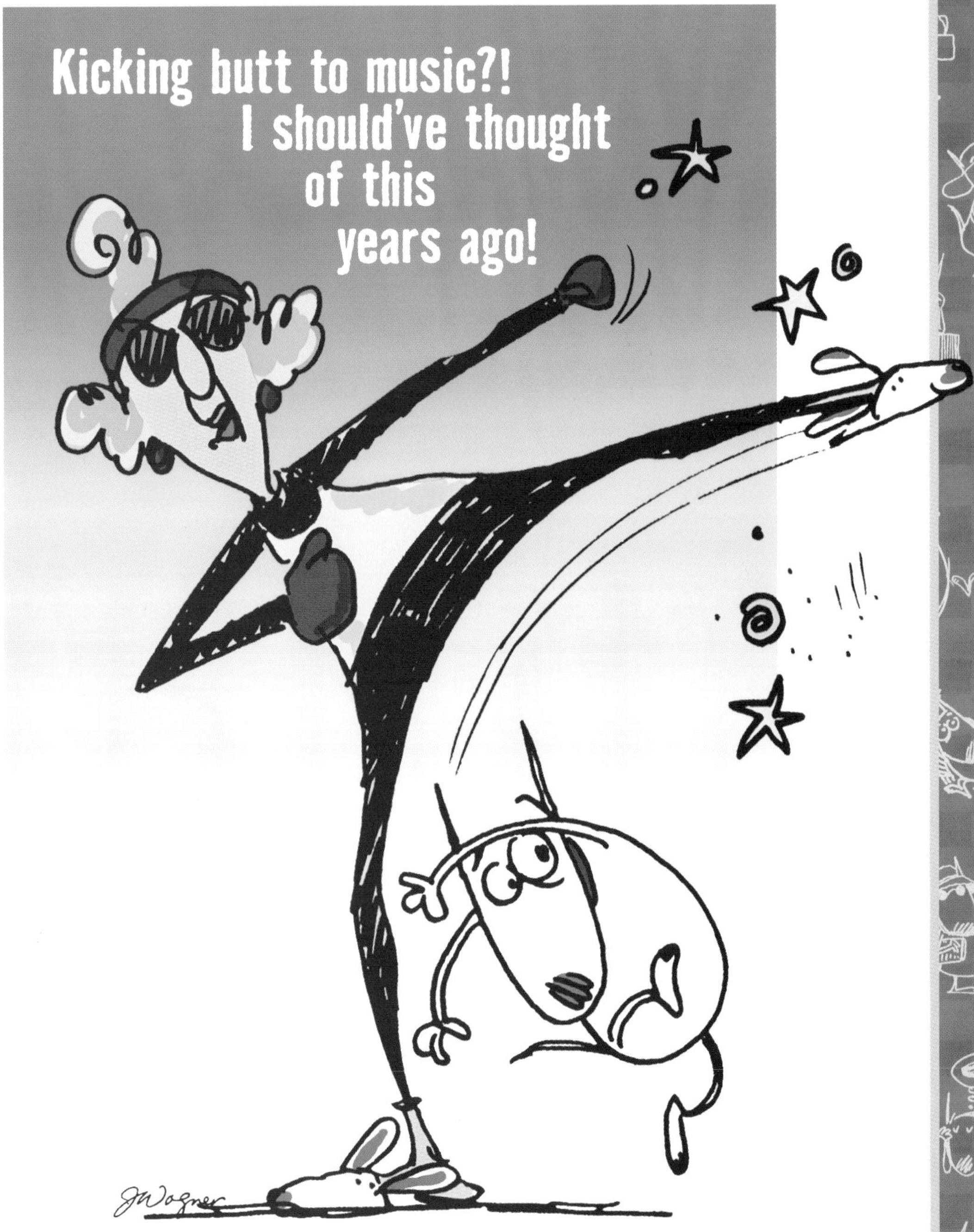
Kicking butt to music?!
I should've thought
of this
years ago!
JWagner

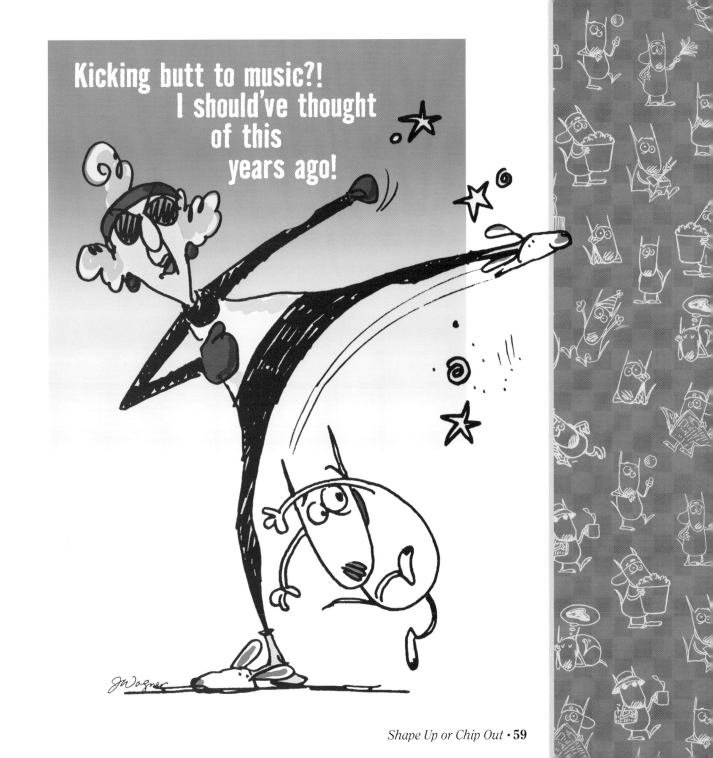

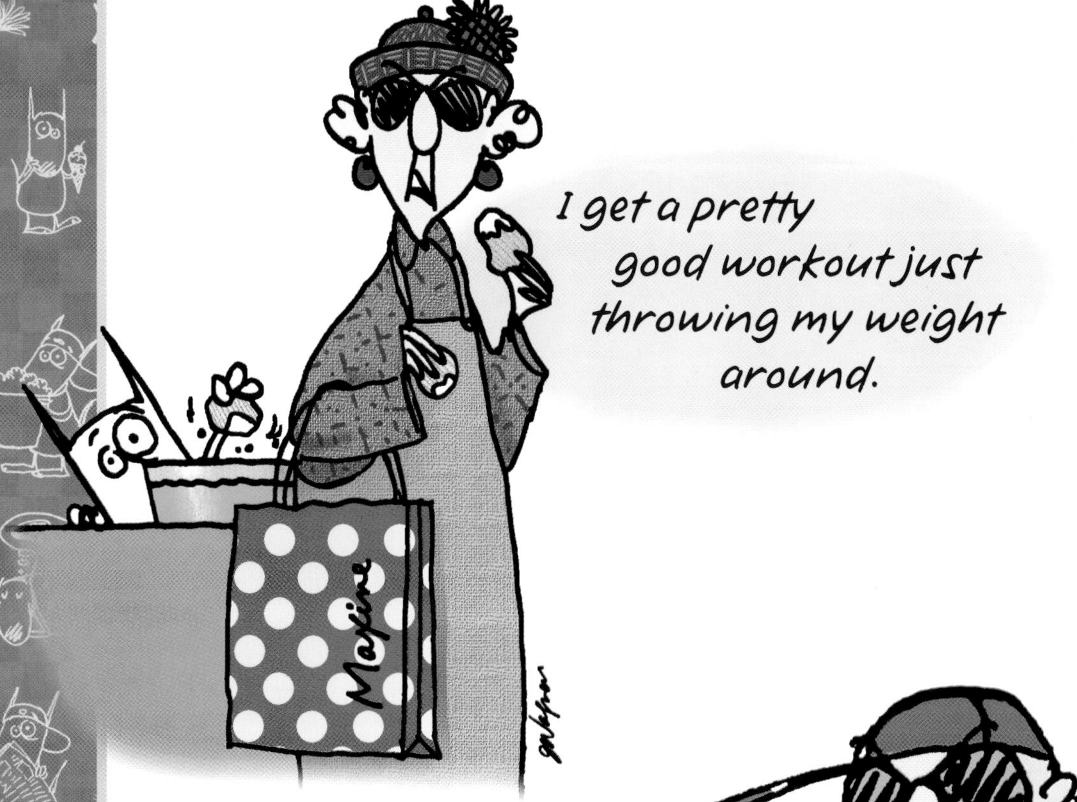
I get a pretty good workout just throwing my weight around.
Maxine

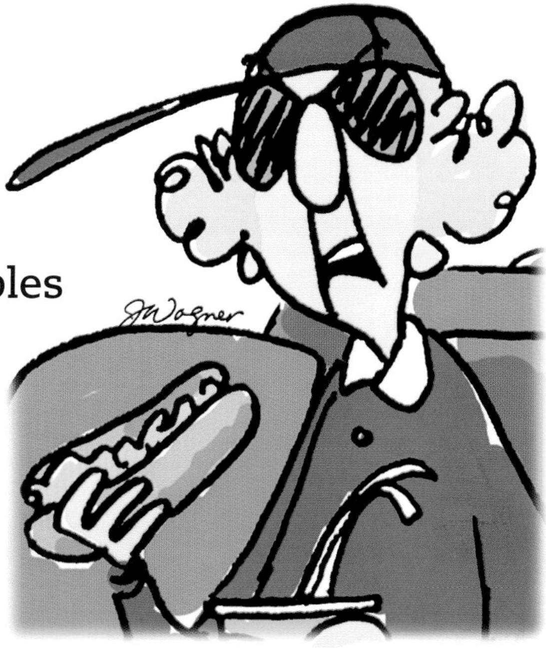
JWagner

I'd eat more fruits and vegetables if they tasted more like microwaved burritos.

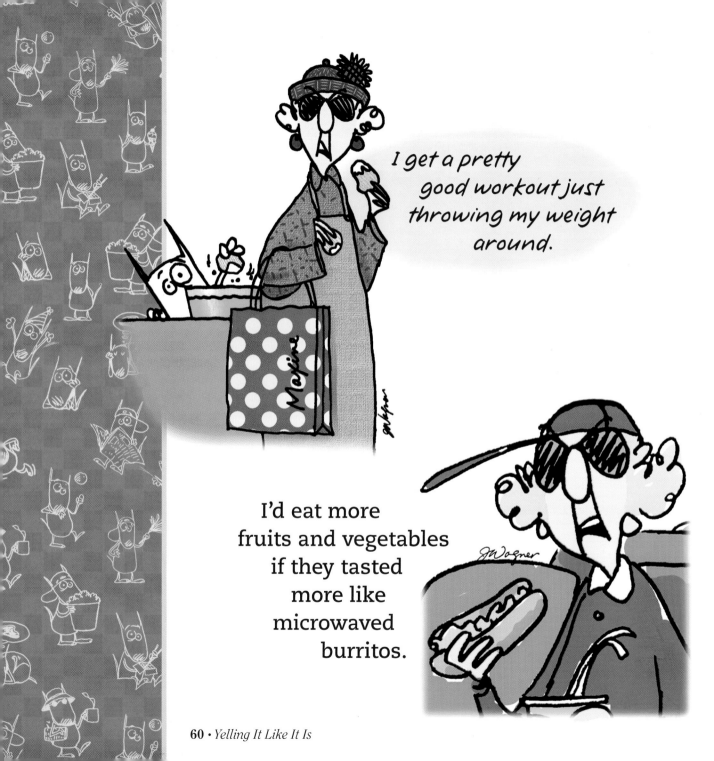

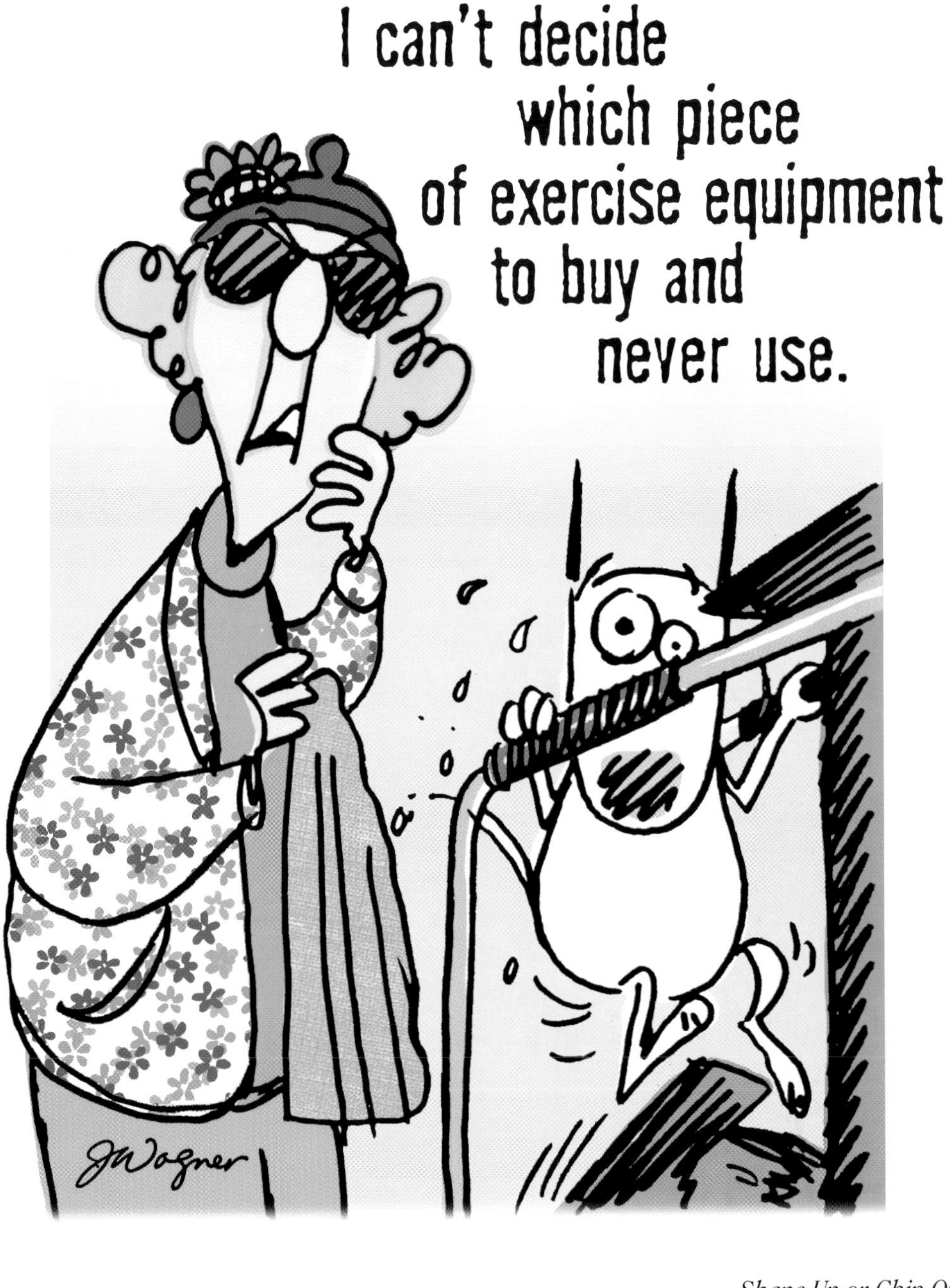
I can't decide which piece of exercise equipment to buy and never use.
JWagner

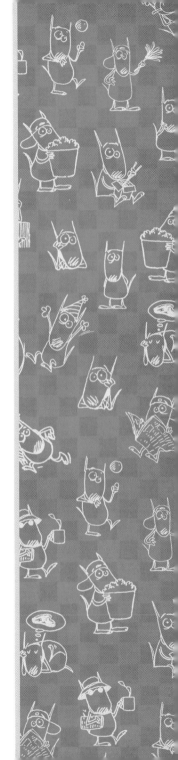

My last good run was in my pantyhose.

I WENT OUT EARLY TO GET the neighbor's paper the other day, and I saw people running down the street. I looked for the rabid dog chasing them or the invading army tanks or something that would make seemingly sane people get up so early and run like crazy people. Turned out they *were* crazy people.

But they weren't the worst. That would be the people who pay upward of a week's worth of groceries to go to a "gym" and "work out." Gym is for fifth-graders who can't figure out how to forge a doctor's note to get out of it. And working out is what you do at anger management classes that the state makes you attend after you... Oh, yeah, the lawyers don't want me talking about that.

I find that exercise helps me relieve stress. I start with a few "butt kicks," then some "middle finger lifts." After that, I wind up with some "mooning for speed and accuracy" reps.

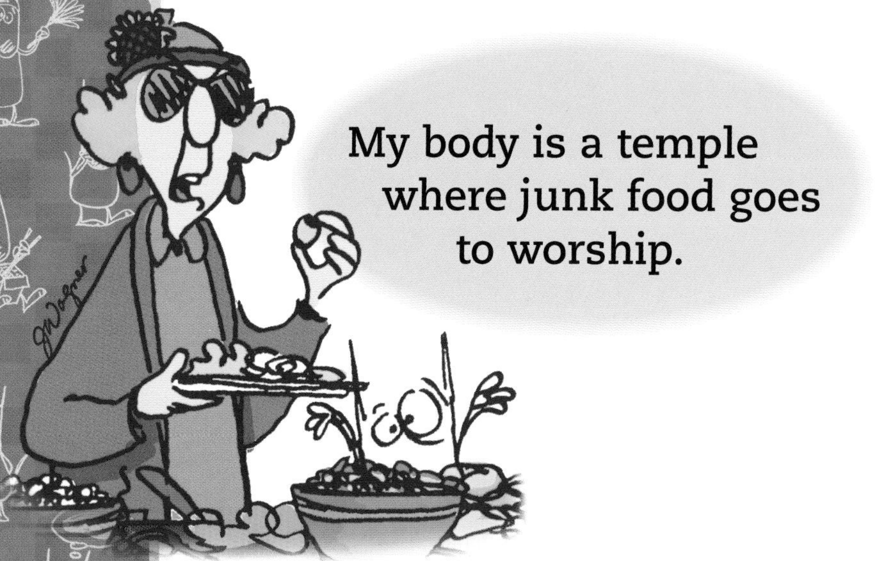
My body is a temple where junk food goes to worship.

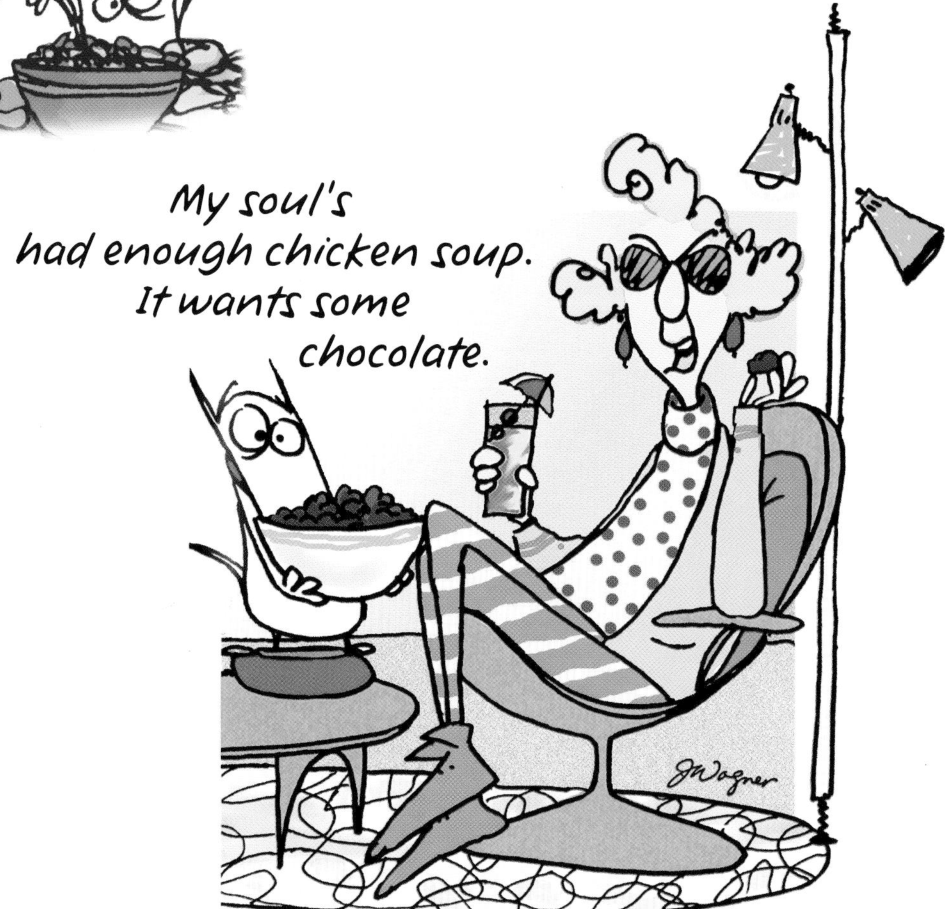
My soul's had enough chicken soup. It wants some chocolate.

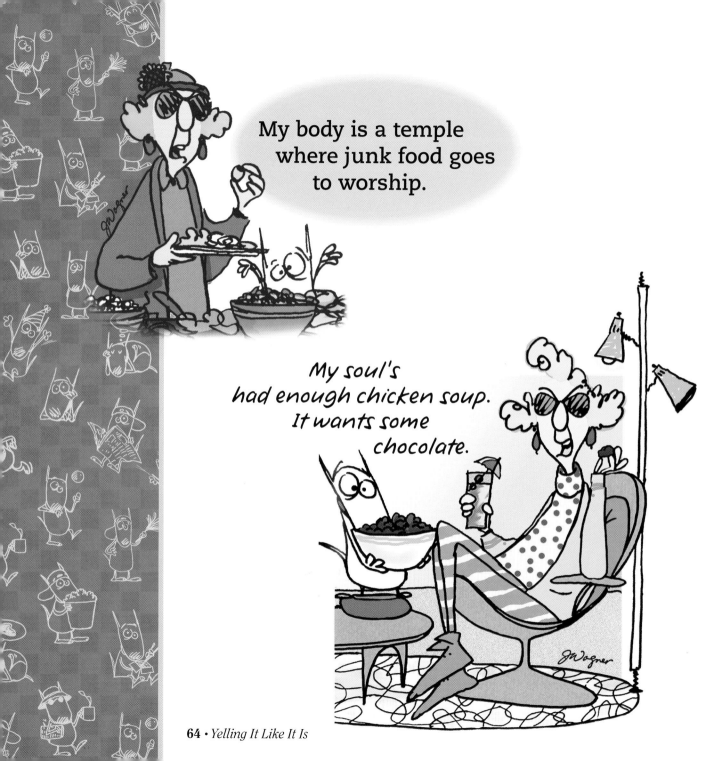

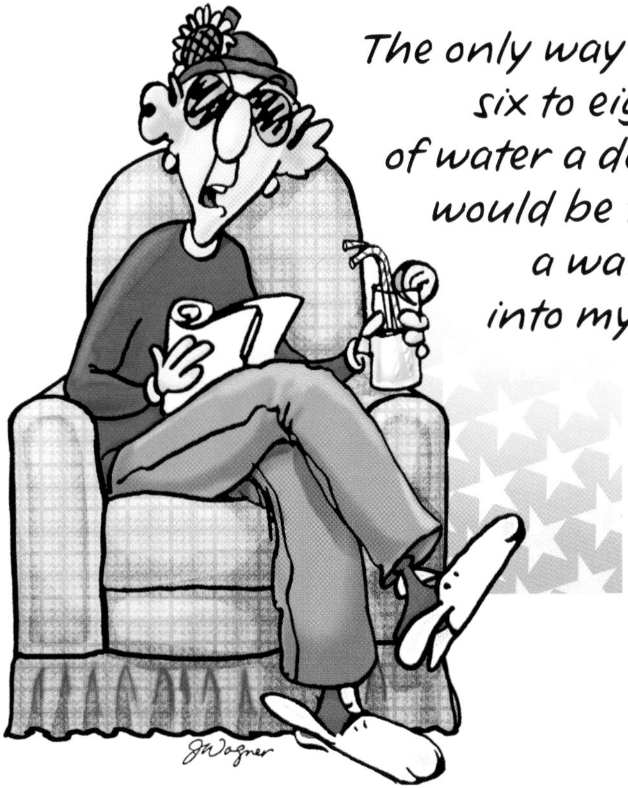

The only way I could drink
six to eight glasses
of water a day
would be to move
a water cooler
into my bathroom.

Know what tastes great
on veggie burgers?

Lettuce, tomato, and beef.

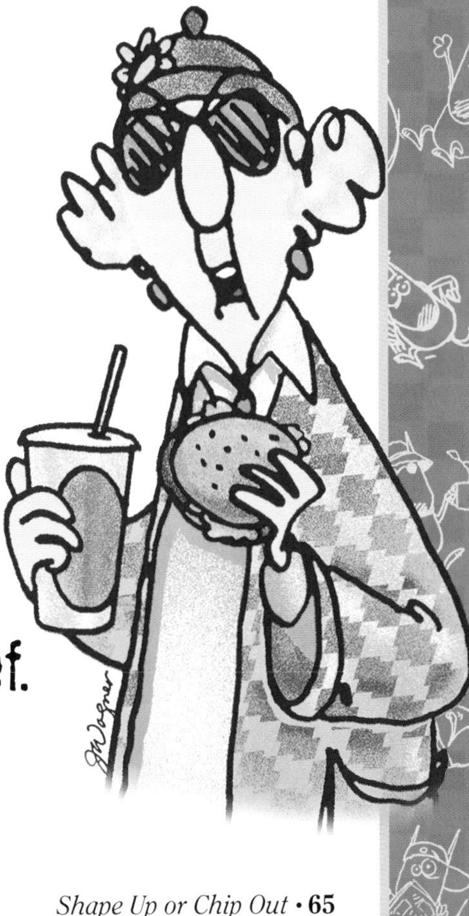

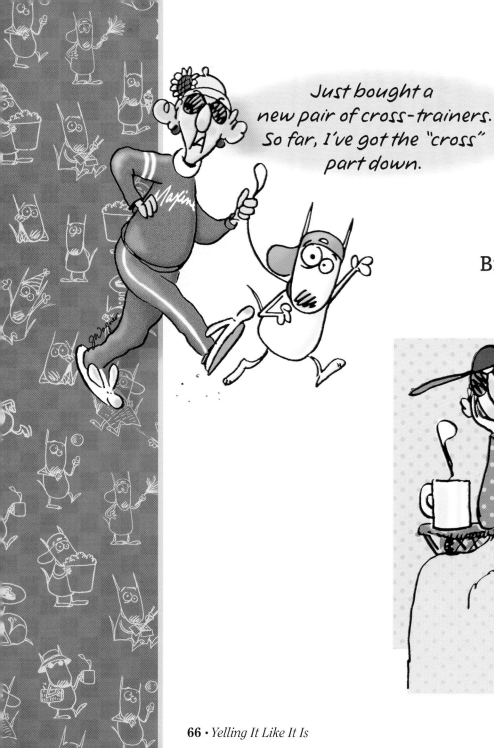

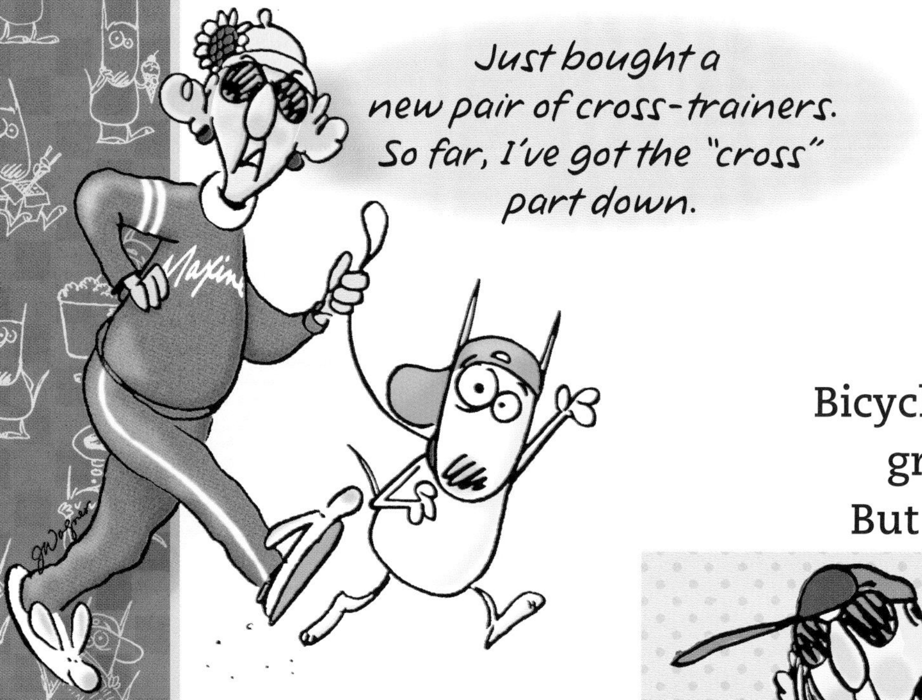
Just bought a new pair of cross-trainers. So far, I've got the "cross" part down.

Bicycling is great exercise. But enough about getting into the shorts.

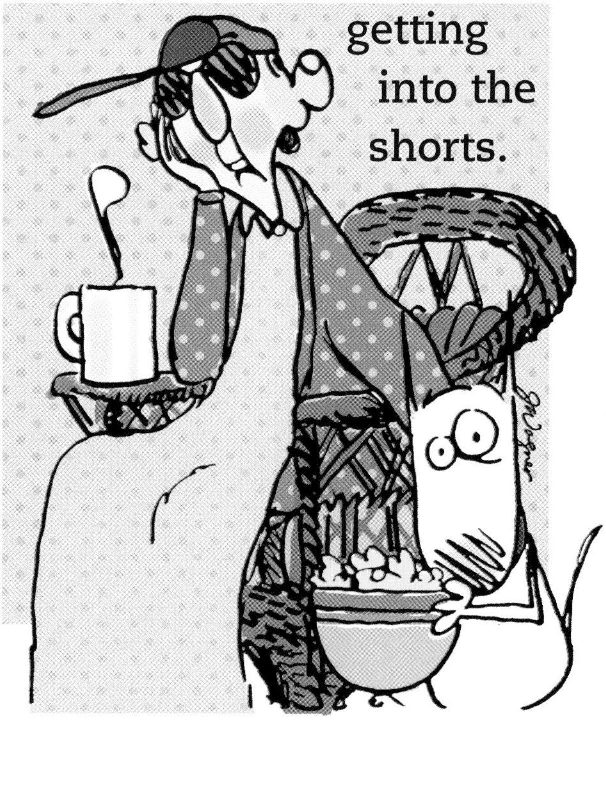

Here's my simple *"get in shape quick"* plan:

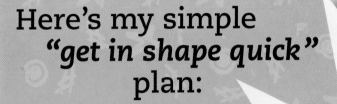

Step one: *Get off your butt.*

Step two: *Move your butt.*

Step three: *Repeat.*

If that doesn't do it,
get used to the shape you have
instead of trying to get
into a new one.

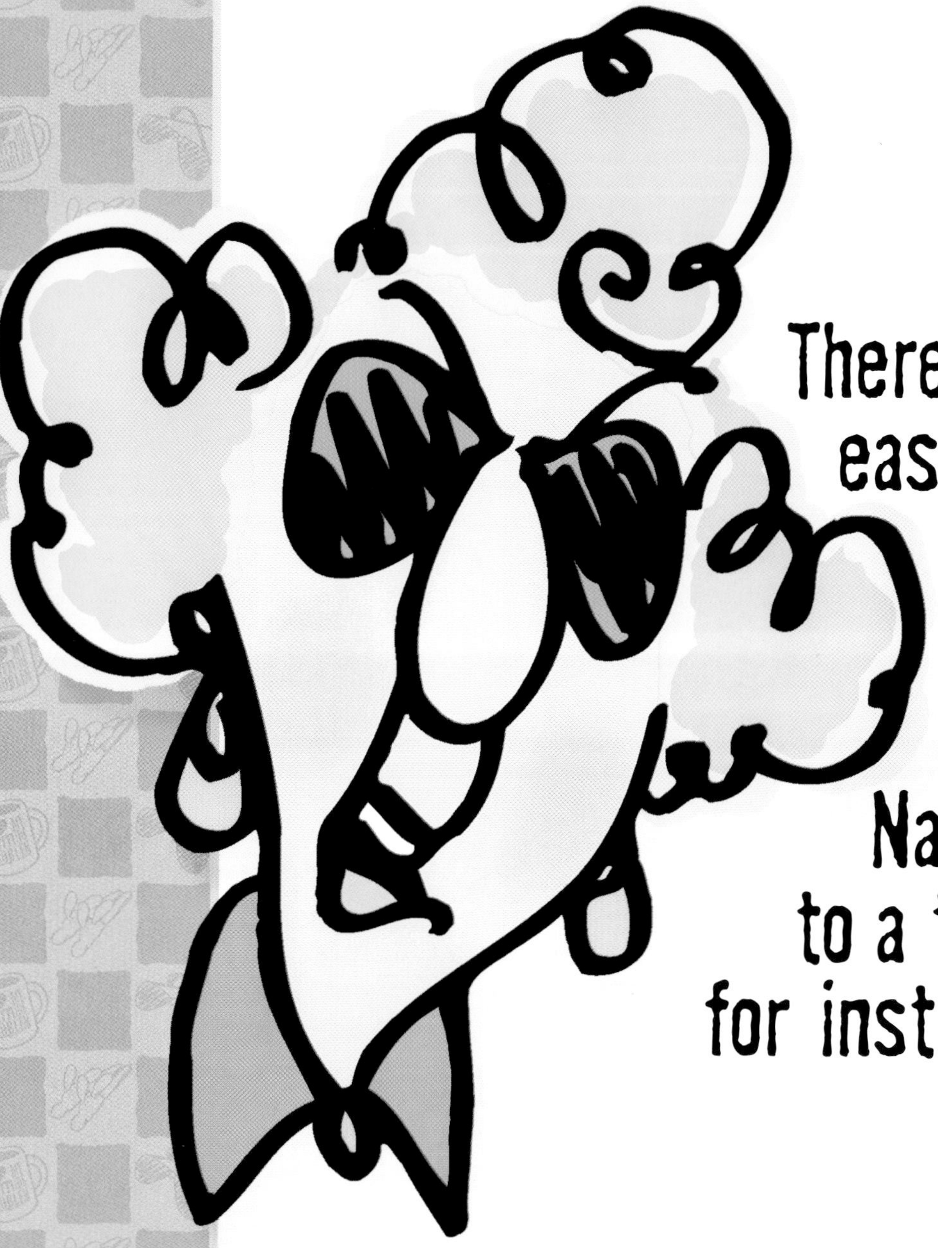

There are
easier things
than
meeting
a good man.
Nailing Jell-O
to a tree,
for instance.

Take the Average Man (Far, Far Away)

DATING IS LIKE RUMMAGING FOR VENDING MACHINE MONEY in the bottom of your purse. After you go through the change, you might forget what you thought you wanted.

I've got my share of gentlemen callers. Mostly aluminum siding guys. They're only interested in one thing. And it's not the thing I'm interested in.

I'm not saying I'm a roaring volcano of passion anymore, but my spark could be fanned into a flame if the right camper came along. All I'm looking for is a guy who'll do what I want, when I want, how I want, for as long as I want, and then go away. Or wait nearby, like a Dust Buster, charged up and ready when needed.

Who wouldn't want a romantic evening of candlelight dining, a walk in the park, slow dancing? Of course, that could all be seriously messed up by a goofball in drawstring pants and a cardigan.

Women don't need the remote control— we have the actual control.

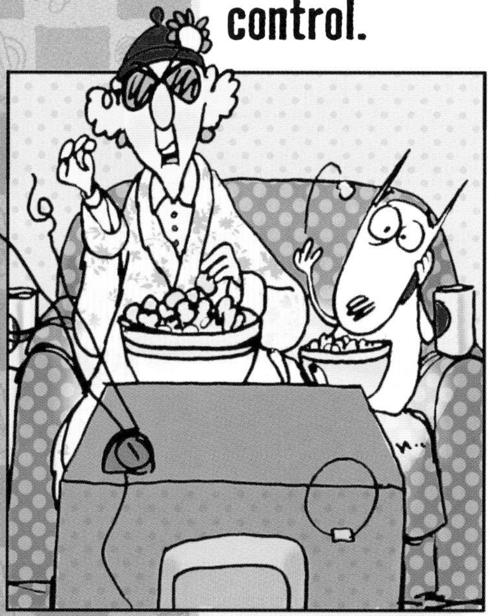

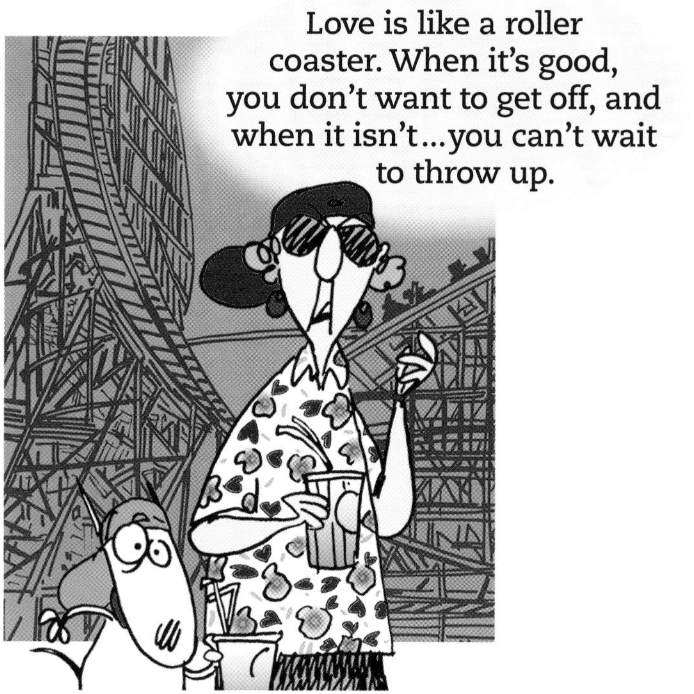
Love is like a roller coaster. When it's good, you don't want to get off, and when it isn't...you can't wait to throw up.

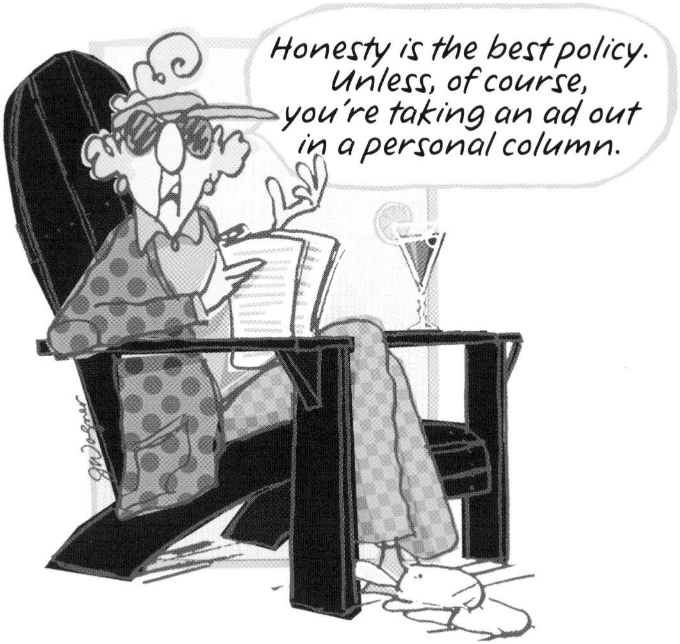
Honesty is the best policy. Unless, of course, you're taking an ad out in a personal column.

Give a man a fish,
and he'll eat for a day.
Teach a man to fish,
and the old buzzard
won't be
hanging around
underfoot
all weekend.

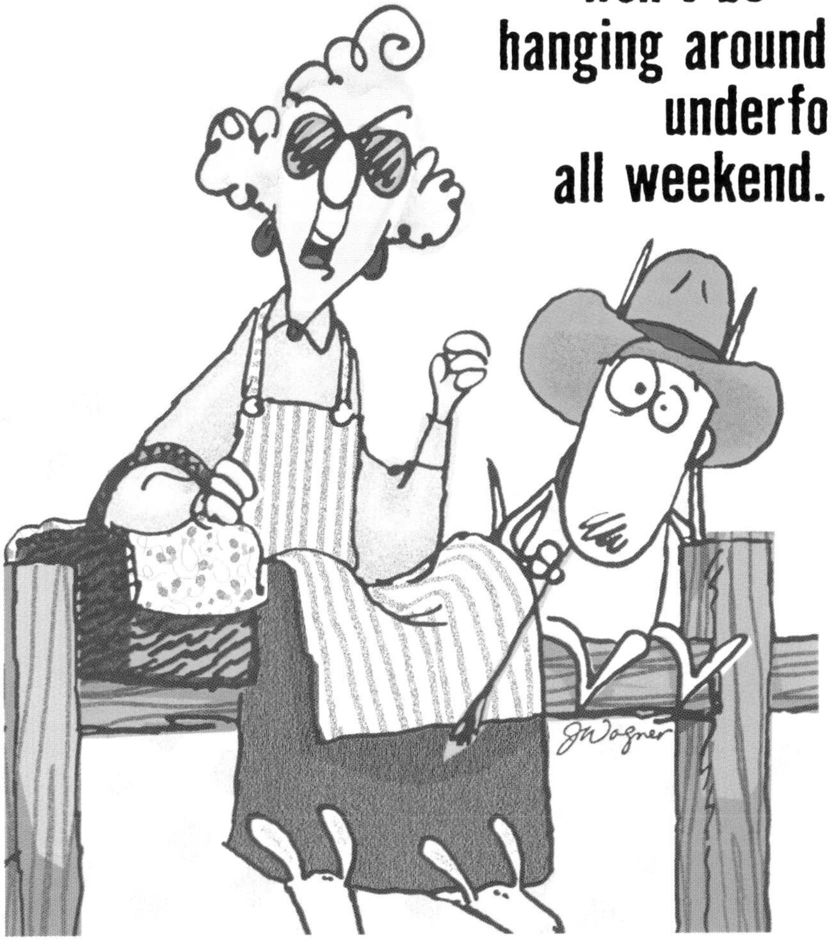
JWagner

YOU'LL NOTICE IT WASN'T A woman who said "I've never met a man I didn't like." I've met several, and believe me, I let 'em know it.

They didn't really mind, though. They were so busy talking about themselves they didn't notice. Call a man in the coldest, most remote part of Alaska, and ask him about surfing. He'll come up with something. And his counterpart on Maui will hold forth on the best way to field-dress a polar bear. That's the way men are. The irony is thick as stubble after a fishing trip, because they're just so wrong about so many things.

The very shape of a sofa would indicate that it was designed to be sat on. Sat. Not laid. Not sprawled. Not slouched. Sat.

Likewise, logic would dictate that your "lucky T-shirt" won't get clean lying on the floor. The toilet paper roll doesn't regenerate, and the toothpaste has a *perfectly good half* on the other side of the Cro-Magnon squeeze in the middle.

Women who think about remarrying
should just throw some
men's underwear on the floor
and shove all the blankets
to the other side
of the bed,
instead.

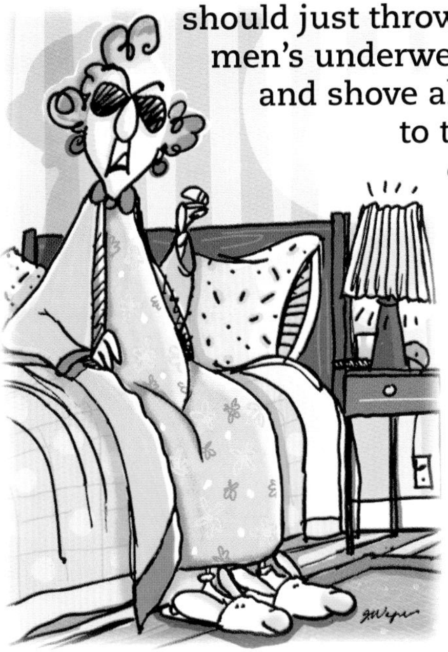

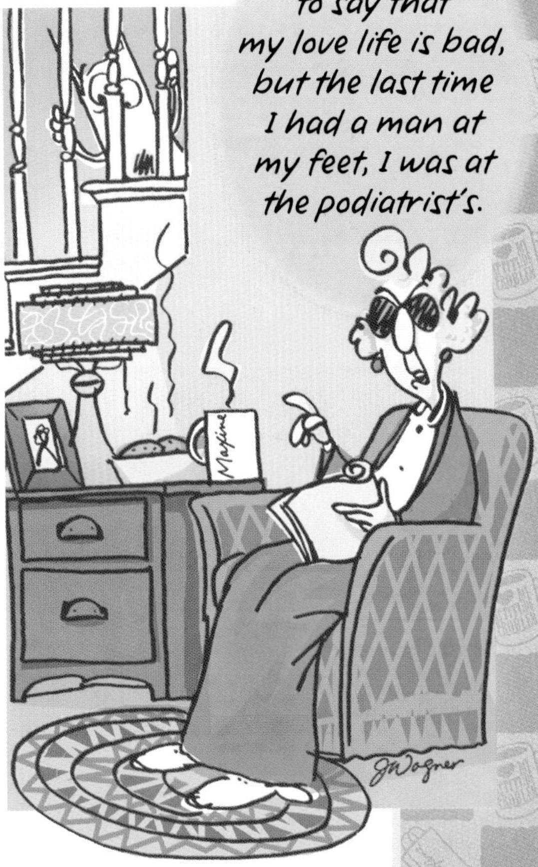
Maxine

I don't want
to say that
my love life is bad,
but the last time
I had a man at
my feet, I was at
the podiatrist's.

I just have three
heartfelt words
for affectionate couples
everywhere–
close the
blinds.

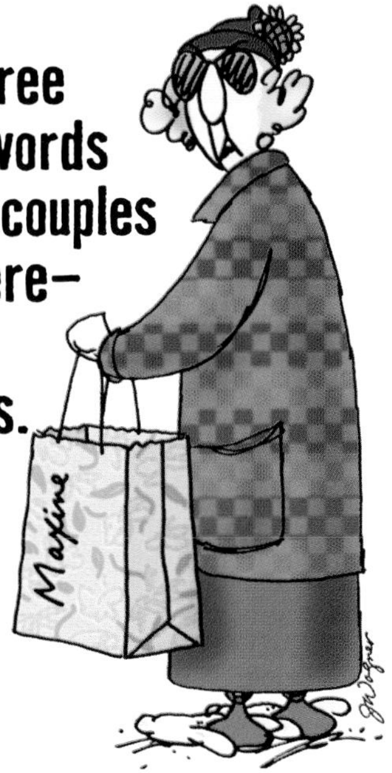
Maxine

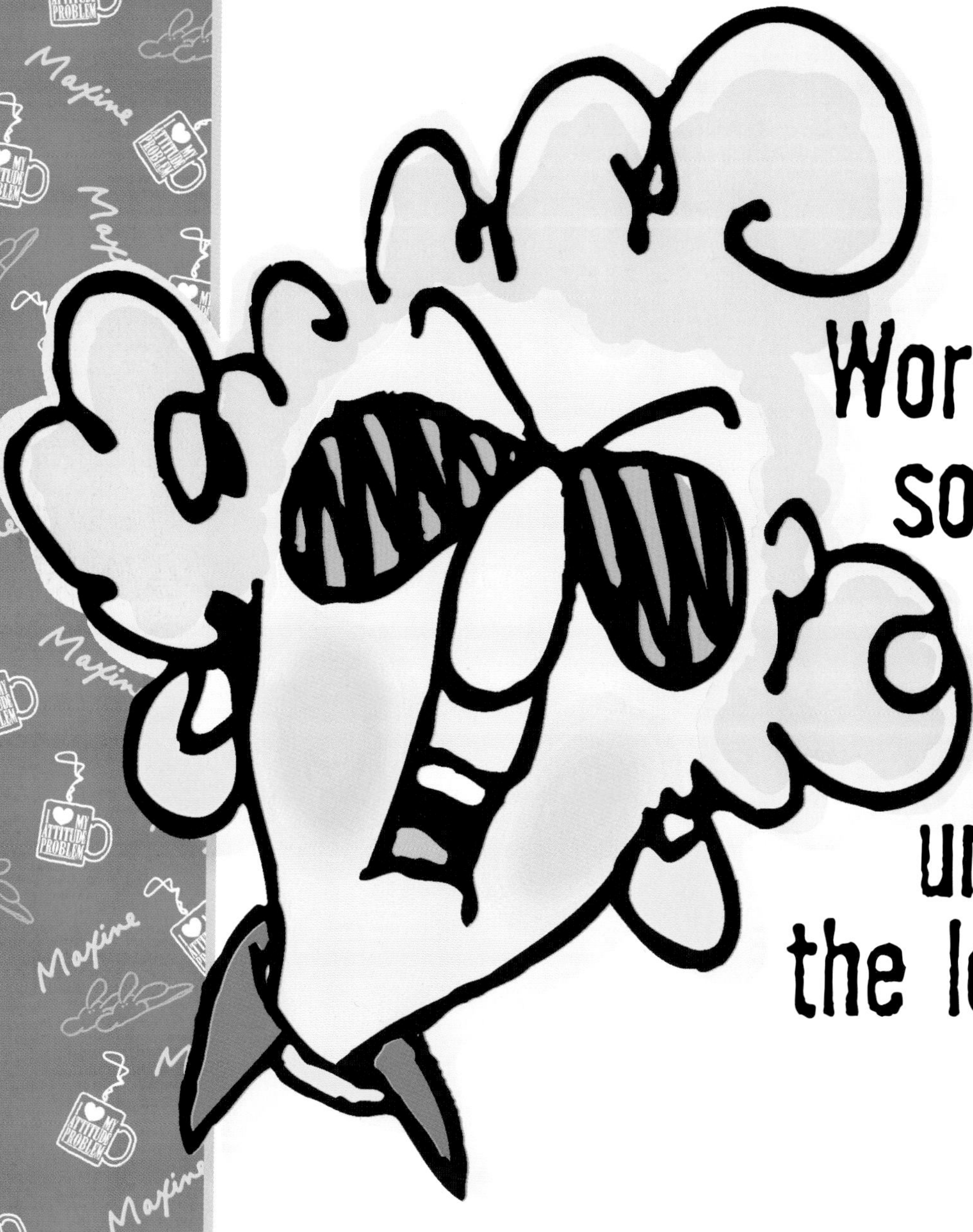

Work is just something I'm doing until I win the lottery.

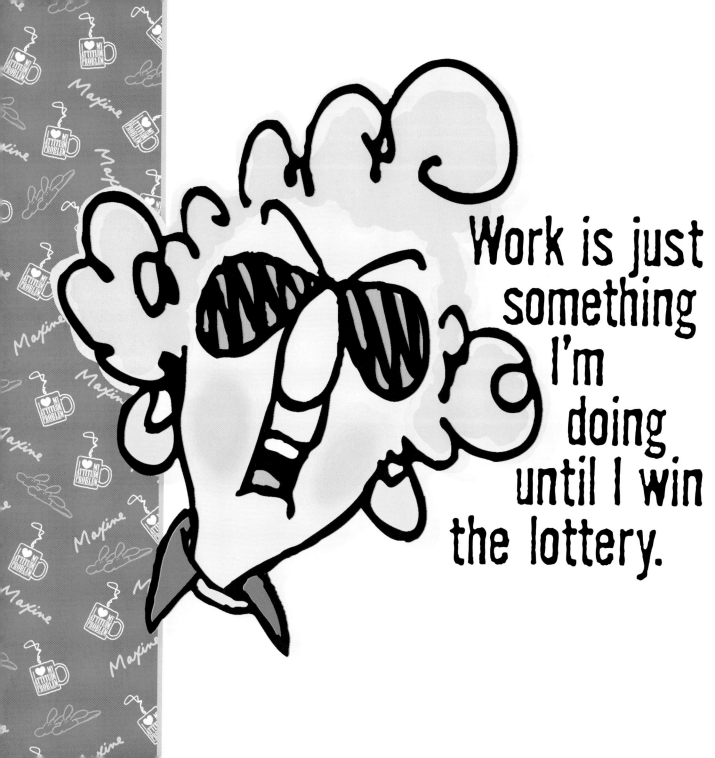

Working Noon Till Five

I BELIEVE IN AN HONEST DAY'S WORK FOR AN HONEST DAY'S pay. I believe in going the extra mile. I believe in putting your nose to the grindstone and giving 110 percent. I've never actually *done* any of those things, but I believe in them.

Now that I think about it, I may not believe in putting your nose to the grindstone. That one just sounds like you're trying to get a cut-rate beak reduction. Sniff with the nose God gave ya, I say.

I'd work hard if I had an employer who cared about me as an individual and, yes, wanted to make a profit, but not at the expense of the most valuable resource–the people. And I'd fly to work every day on my invisible dragon and have him heat up my sloppy joe with fire from his nostrils, because I'd be living in dreamland.

There's a lot to be said for hardworkin' stiffs who punch a clock. Mainly, they should get a less violent habit. You can really hurt yourself taking it out on a Timex. And I understand that white-collar workers put in a tough day, too. Or I understand that they think they do. Seriously, I've got a lot of respect for our society's paper pushers. Without them, what would the lawyers do? When I make a Power Point presentation, it only takes a finger.

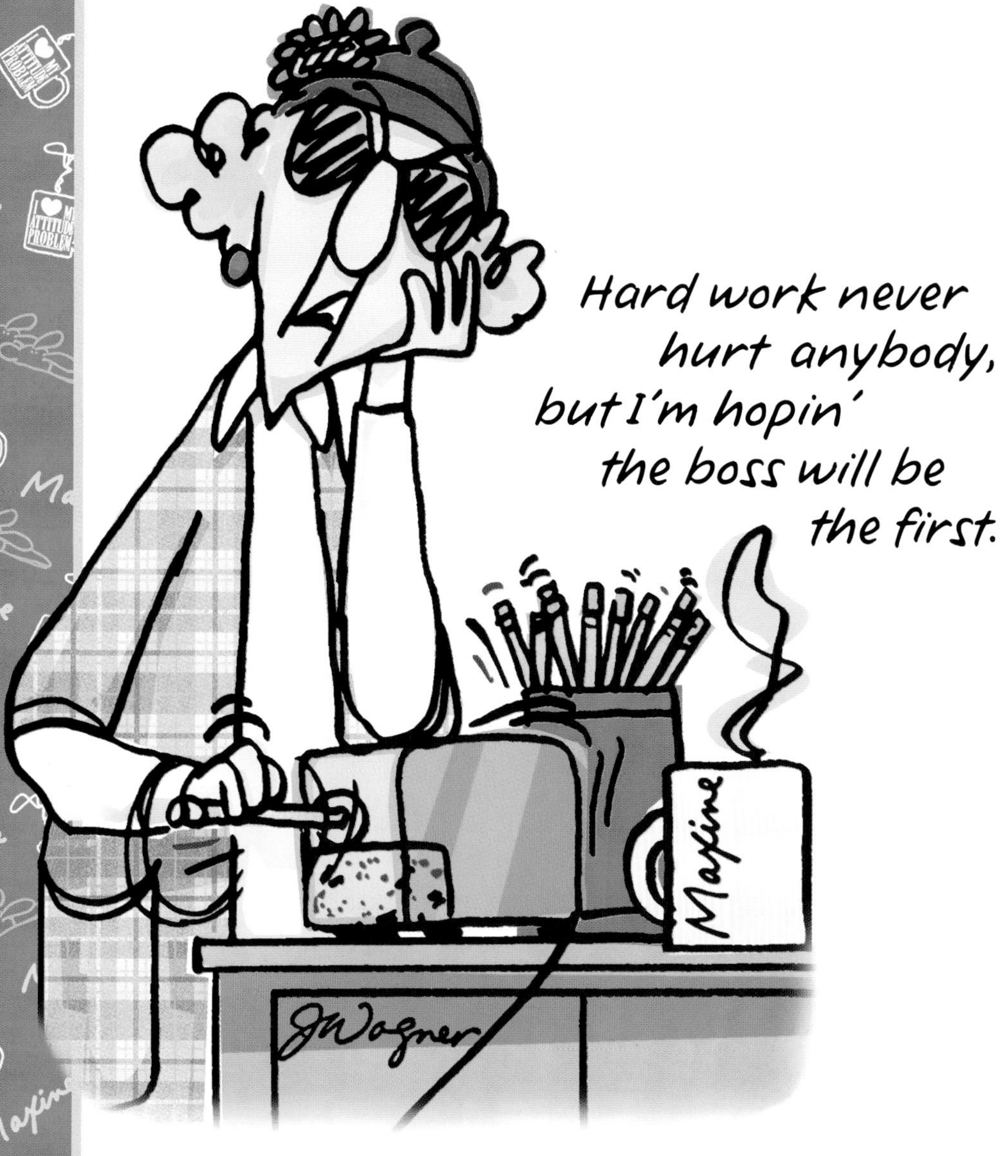
Hard work never hurt anybody, but I'm hopin' the boss will be the first.
Maxine

They created
a new department to
simplify things at the office.
Oh, to be kidding...

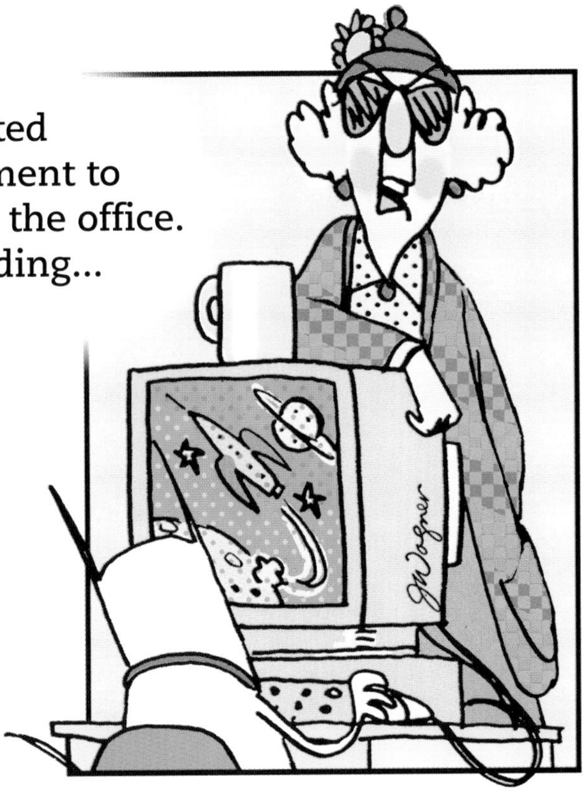

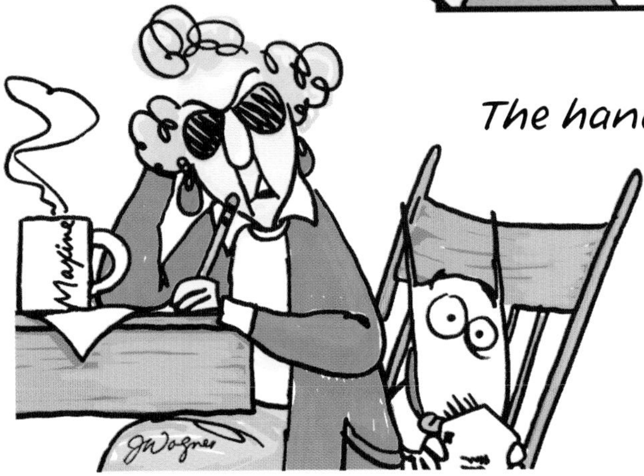
Maxine

The handy thing about my job? I can count the benefits on one finger.

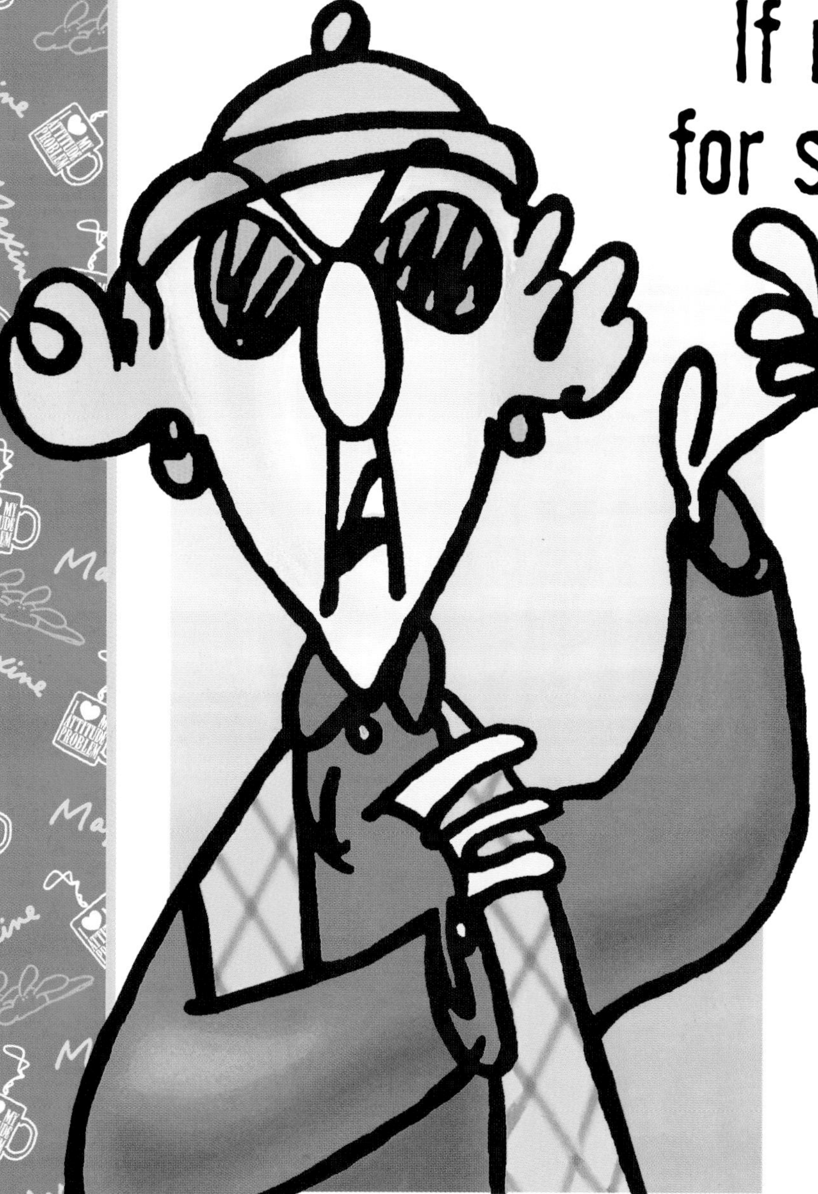

If not
for stress,
I'd have
no energy
at all.

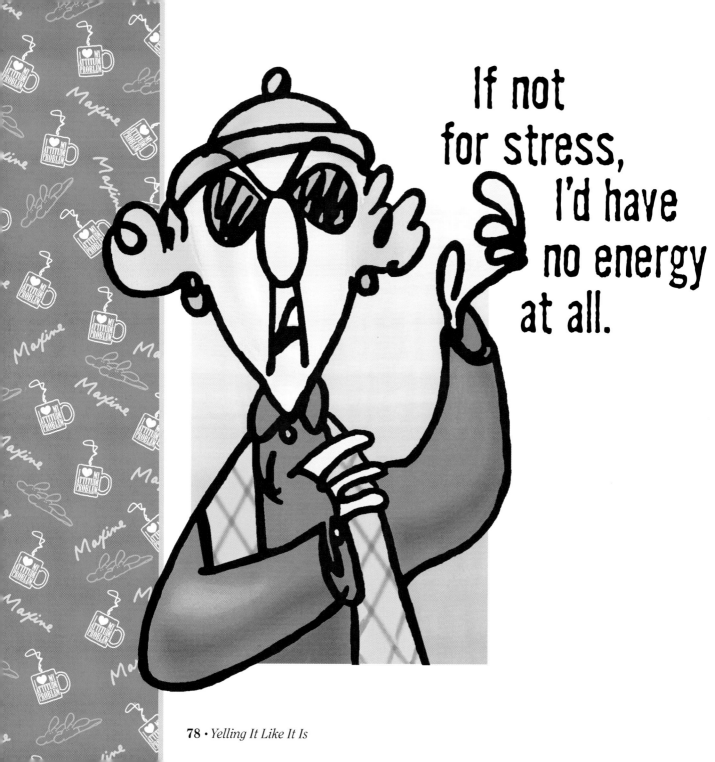

I make it a policy to never take work home with me...unless office supplies count.

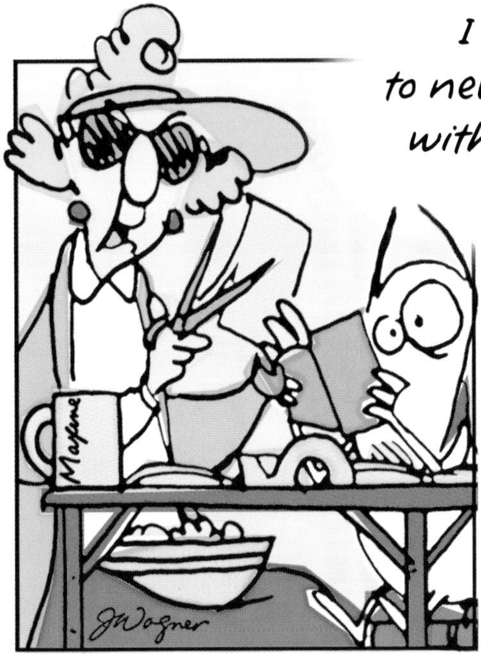
Maxine

I'm not so much goofing off as impersonating upper management.

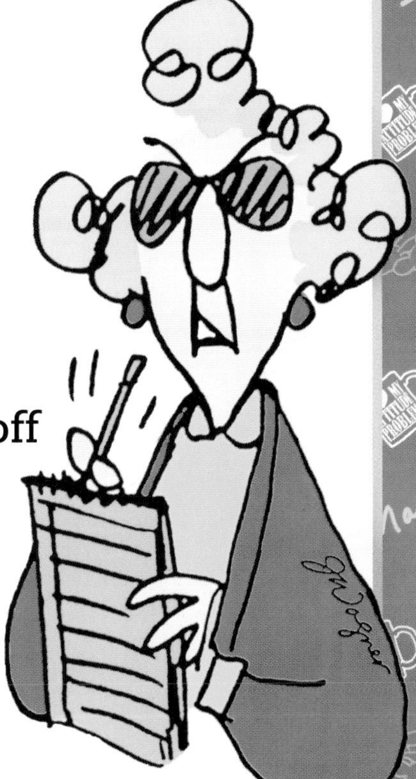

I always work as
if I owned
the business.
Turns out I'm a
lazy owner
who just doesn't care
if the whole
thing
goes down
the tubes.

My idea of rebooting is kicking somebody in the butt twice.

IT'S NO COINCIDENCE THAT YOU can't spell "compost" without most of the letters in "computers." These techno-ill-logical wonders make it easier and faster for the modern worker to get in touch with lots of free-floating anger and not a small amount of rage.

I guess computers wouldn't bug me if they ever worked, so in that way, they're like most of my relatives. They lie around on furniture, make strange noises, and don't produce anything. Hmm...maybe some of the relatives *are* computers. Nah, that'd be interesting.

The worst thing about people at the office being replaced by computers is that computers don't respond to threats.

I ♥ MY ATTITUDE PROBLEM
Maxine

My performance at work has really improved over the years. Now I can nail a moving co-worker with a paper clip shot from a rubber band at 20 yards.
I ♥ MY ATTITUDE PROBLEM
JWagner

CO-WORKERS ARE LIKE leprechauns. I've heard of them, I've seen pictures, but I've never seen one in person. Oh, I've worked near people, but they didn't seem to be working at all. They were only "co." In fact, the harder I worked, the less the co's did.

Co-retirees, I've seen–but co-workers, not so much. I suppose they're out there somewhere with the "money-back guarantee" and the "one-size-fits-all pantyhose."

I file everything
under "F" for
"Forget about it!"

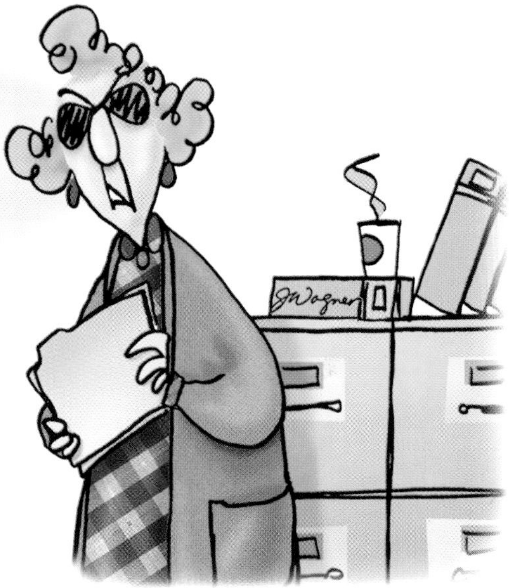

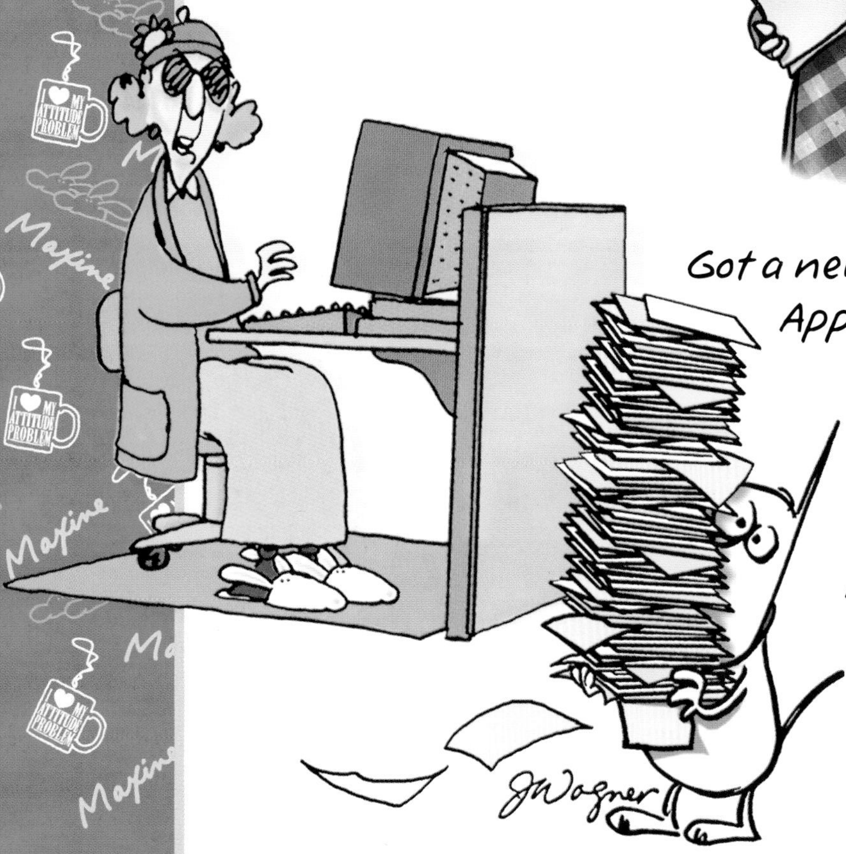

Got a new supervisor.
Apparently,
they
shipped
the last
monkey
back to
the zoo.

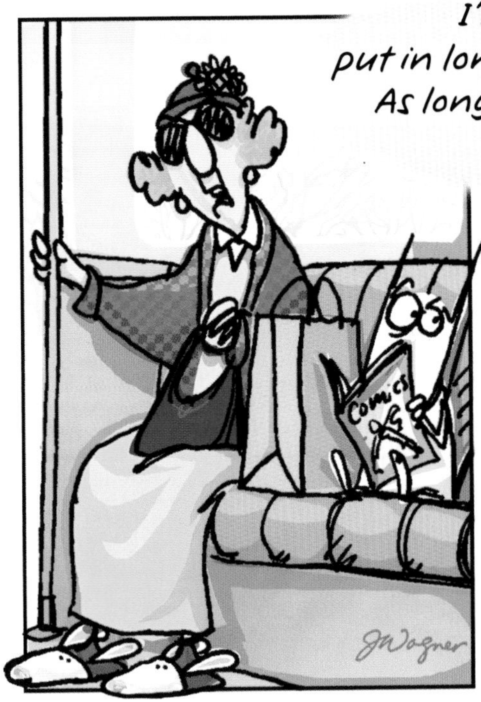
COMICS
JWagner

I'm willing to put in longer hours at work. As long as they're lunch hours.

**I'm not a slacker—
I just don't find work
that riveting.**

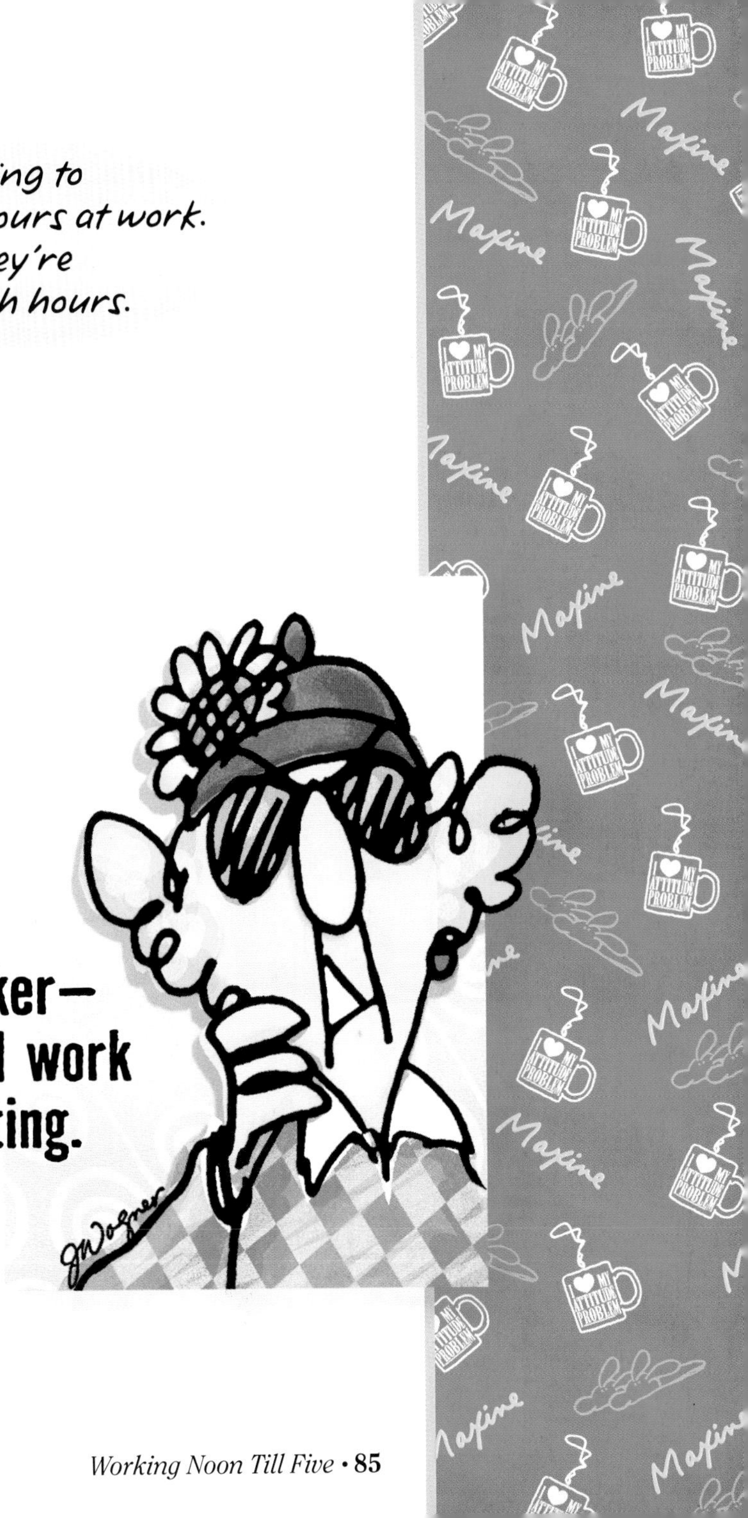
JWagner

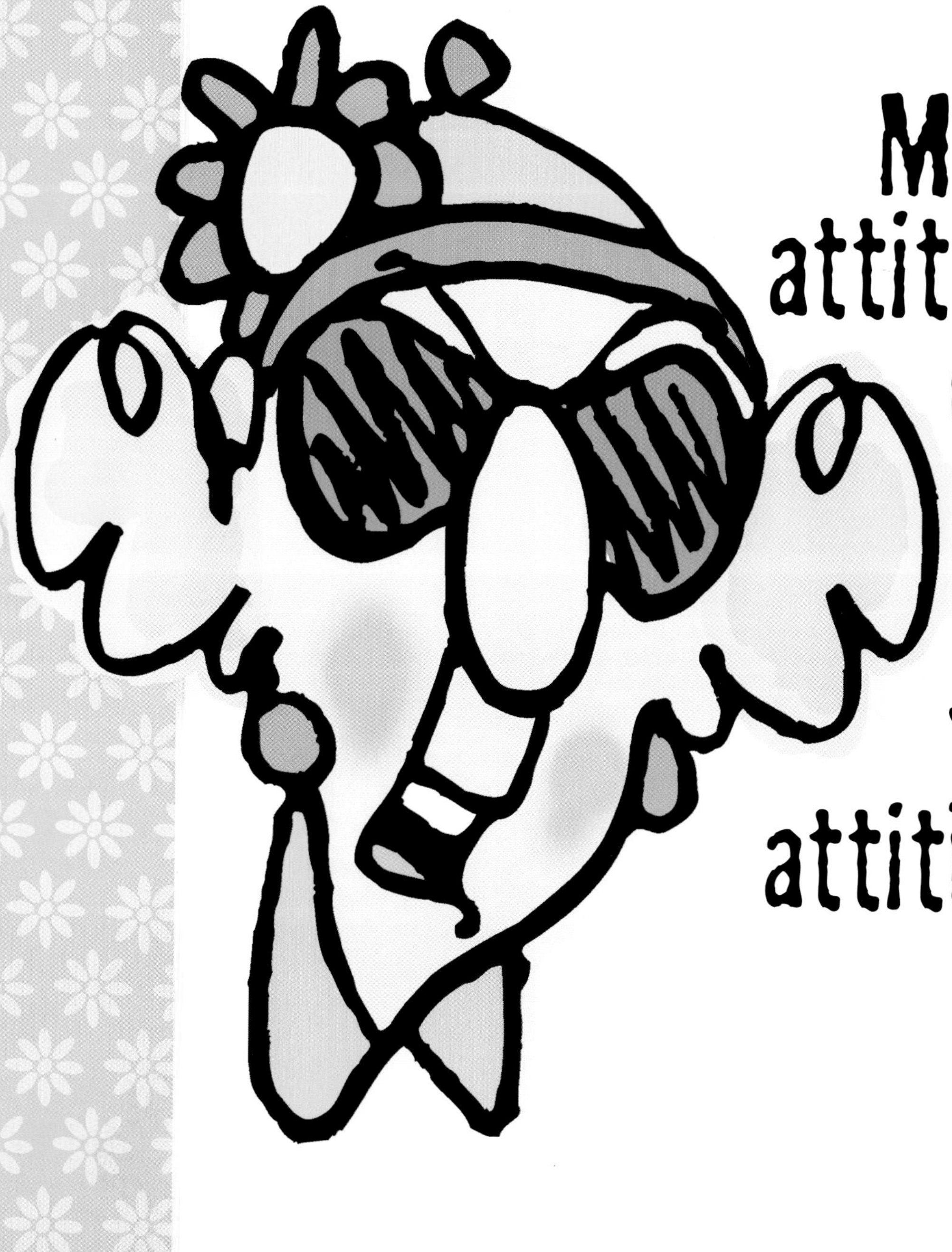

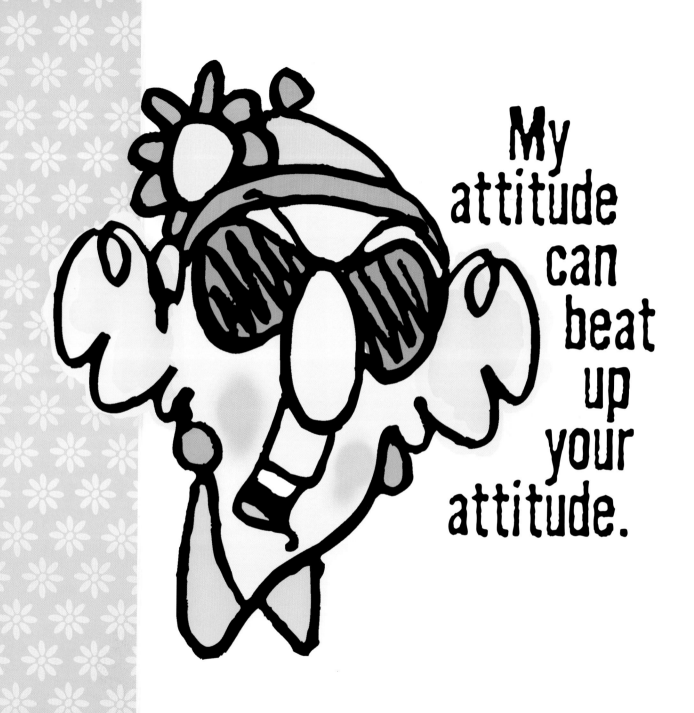

My
attitude
can
beat
up
your
attitude.

Cut the Crap 101

WHEN YOU'RE AN INTERNATIONAL ICON AND A ROLE MODEL to millions, people want to know your secret.

My secret is that there is no secret. I shoot from the plastic hip and let the chumps fall where they may. I call 'em as I squint at 'em. It's my way or, well...it's *just* my way.

At the same time, I always try to remember the little people. Since seniors tend to shrink, I'll be one someday. I never kick someone who's down. Especially if I kicked 'em down in the first place.

Years ago, I learned that you catch more flies with honey than by chasing them around the kitchen with a fire hose you illegally hooked to the hydrant in front of your house.

Also, it takes more muscles to frown than to pretend you can't hear and make the person say things over and over while you laugh real hard on the inside.

If you need
a shoulder
to cry on,
pull off to the side
of the road.

NEVER IN THE HISTORY OF THE WORLD (AND I WAS HERE for most of it, so I know) have so many people whined so much about so little.

Serfs who farmed mud and were considered old-timers at 27 didn't complain like people do today.

Millionaires who became paupers overnight during the Great Depression didn't bellyache. Today Wall Streeters whine about losing a thousandth of a percent on a tech stock. *It was called the* Great Depression, *and they didn't whine.*

You have a lover but not a soul mate, you don't have the calves of a dancer, your hair shines but not like you want it to shine, your car phone is hard to hear over the ten-CD changer, and that kid at the coffee place *knows* you said "no nutmeg," and that's nutmeg floating in the whipped cream, isn't it? Isn't it?!

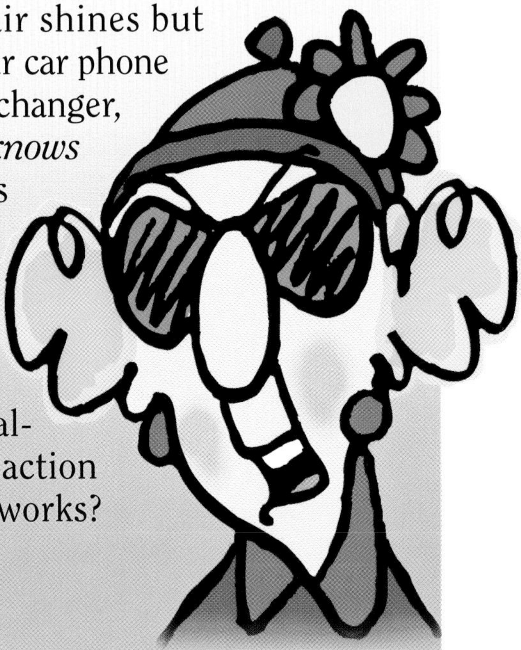

I have no sympathy for whiners. On the other hand, I do have one of those industrial-strength, turbocharged, pump-action squirt guns. Wanna see how it works? Keep talkin'.

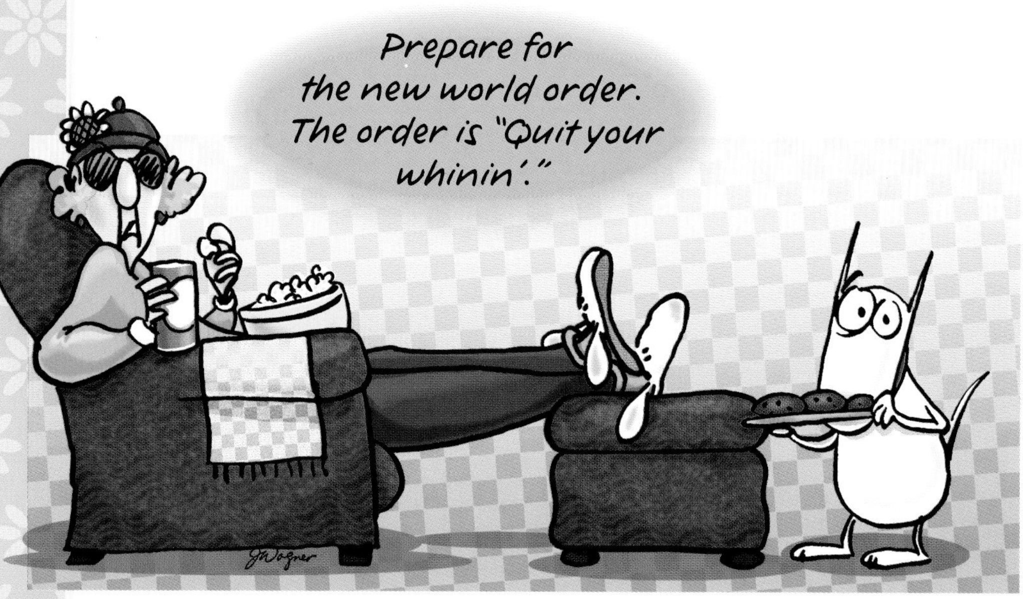
Prepare for the new world order. The order is "Quit your whinin'."

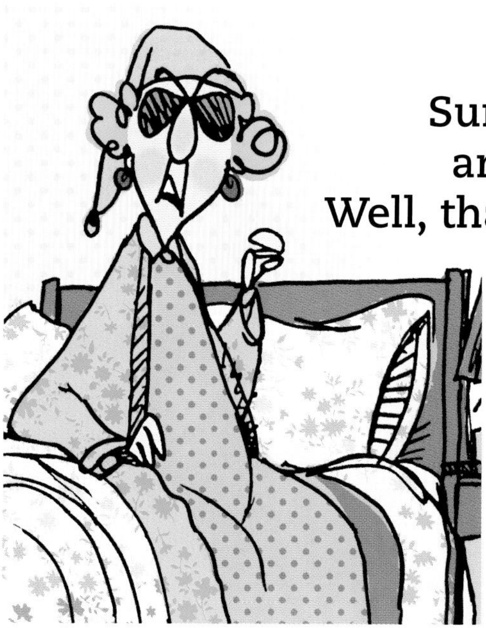

Sunsets, rainbows,
and baby chicks.
Well, that's all the fuzzy crap
I know.
I'm tapped out.

All I want is a little understanding.
Like, when I say
"Get lost, pal!"
I really want you
to understand
that.

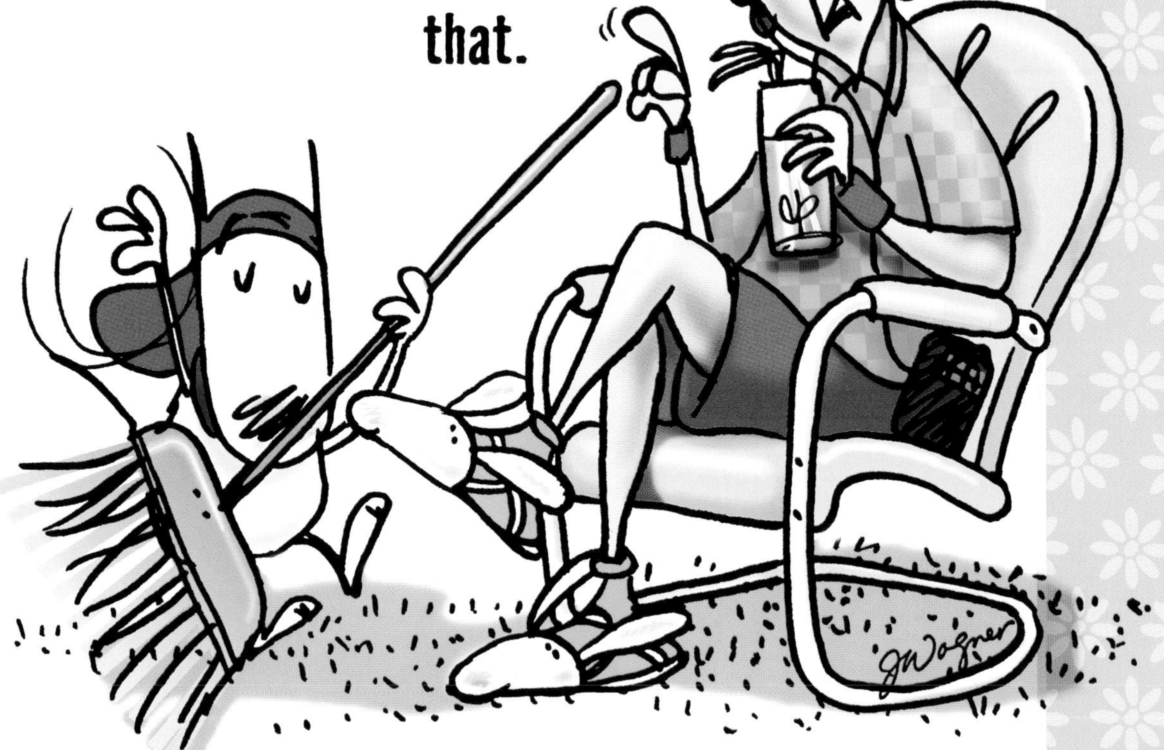

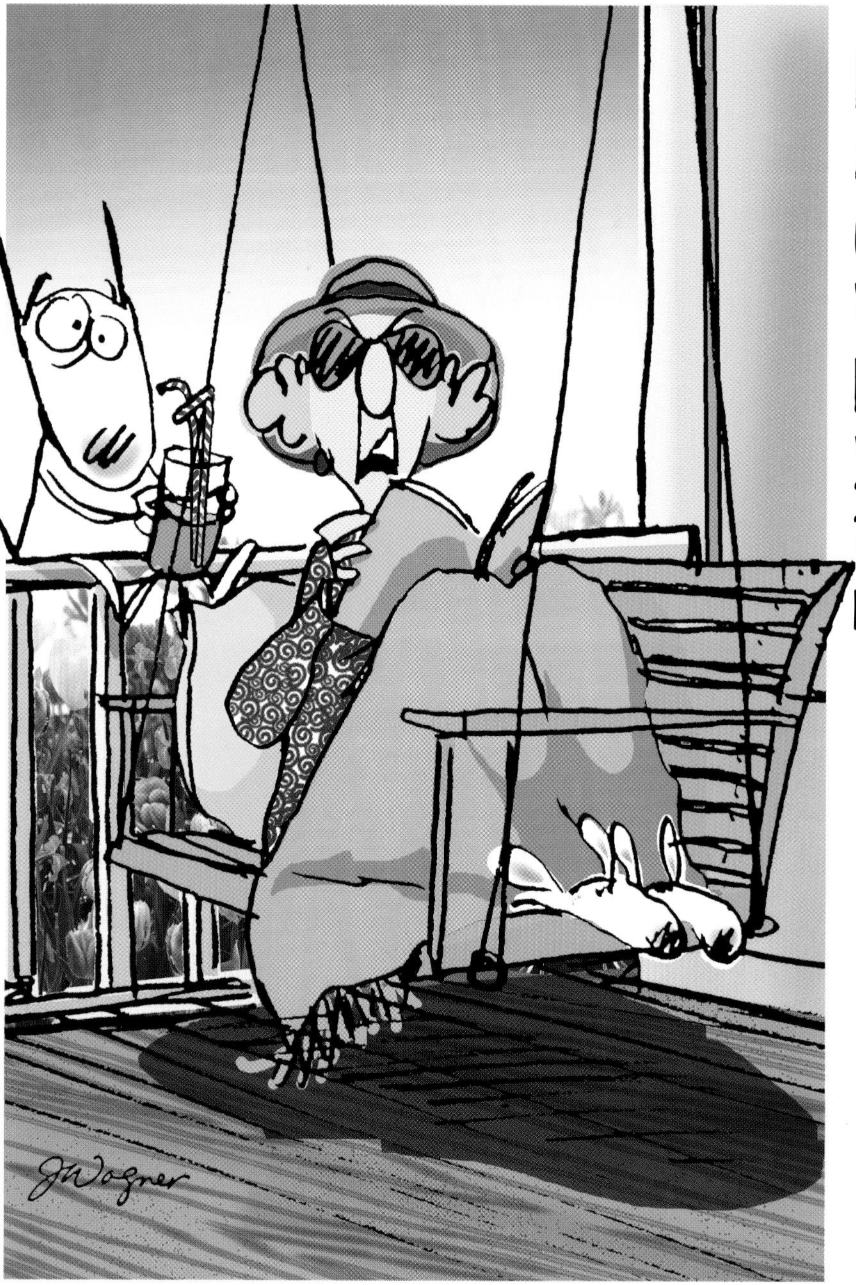

JWagner

Having a bad day? Well, better you than me.

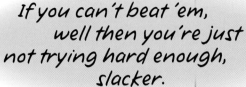

If you can't beat 'em, well then you're just not trying hard enough, slacker.

Ever notice how people who tell you to calm down are the ones who got you mad in the first place?

When the world deals you a lemon,
do what I do–
make whiskey sours!

*Happiness
is where
you find it.
Perhaps you
should look
someplace else.*

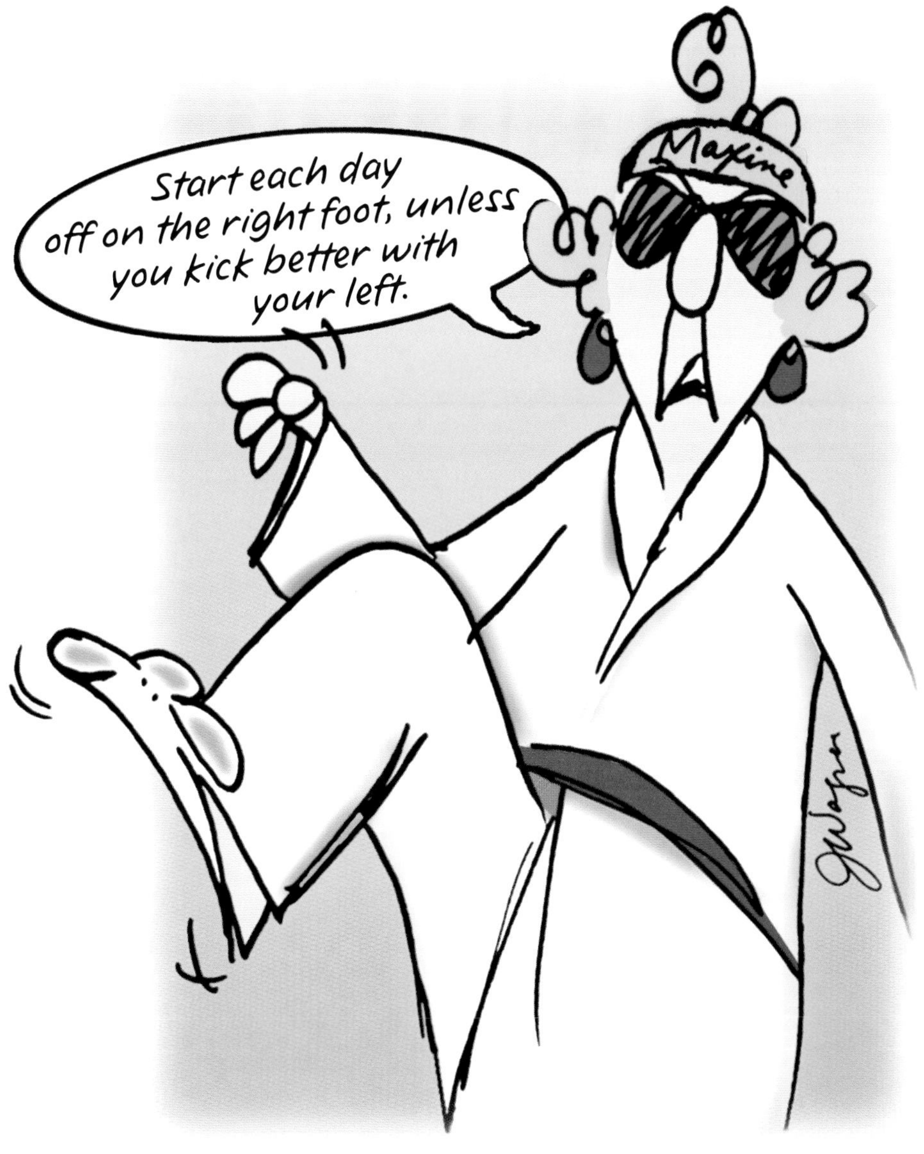
Start each day off on the right foot, unless you kick better with your left.
Maxine

TELL IT LIKE IT IS

Next time
you hear an
eternal optimist
spewing
proverbial sayings,
be prepared
with one
of my favorite crabby
retorts.

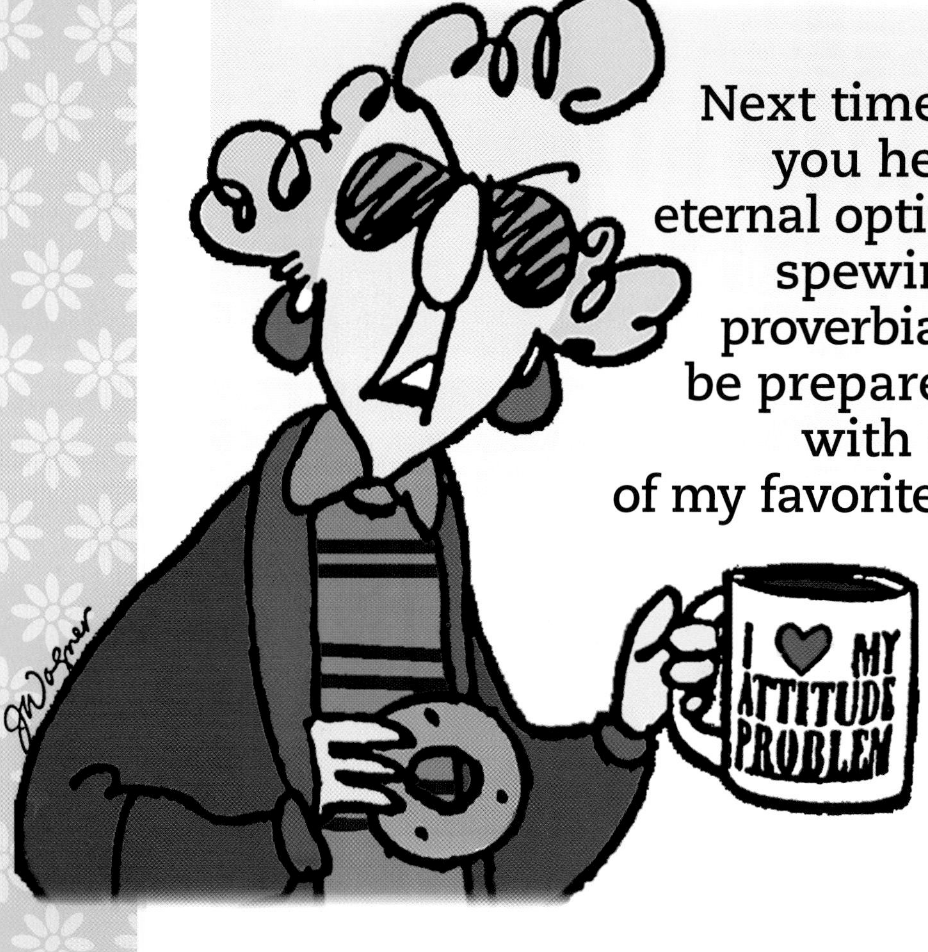
I ♥ MY ATTITUDE PROBLEM
JWagner

When the Eternal Optimist Says:	You Say:
Remember, there's always a silver lining.	In my case, it's usually loose hairs.
If you don't have anything nice to say, don't say anything.	Just make a crude gesture.
Love makes the world go round.	And my lunch come back up.
It takes fewer muscles to smile than to frown.	And fewer still to ignore somebody completely.
Have a good weekend!	Oh, thanks! If you hadn't said that, who knows what kind of terrible time I might have had! I owe ya!

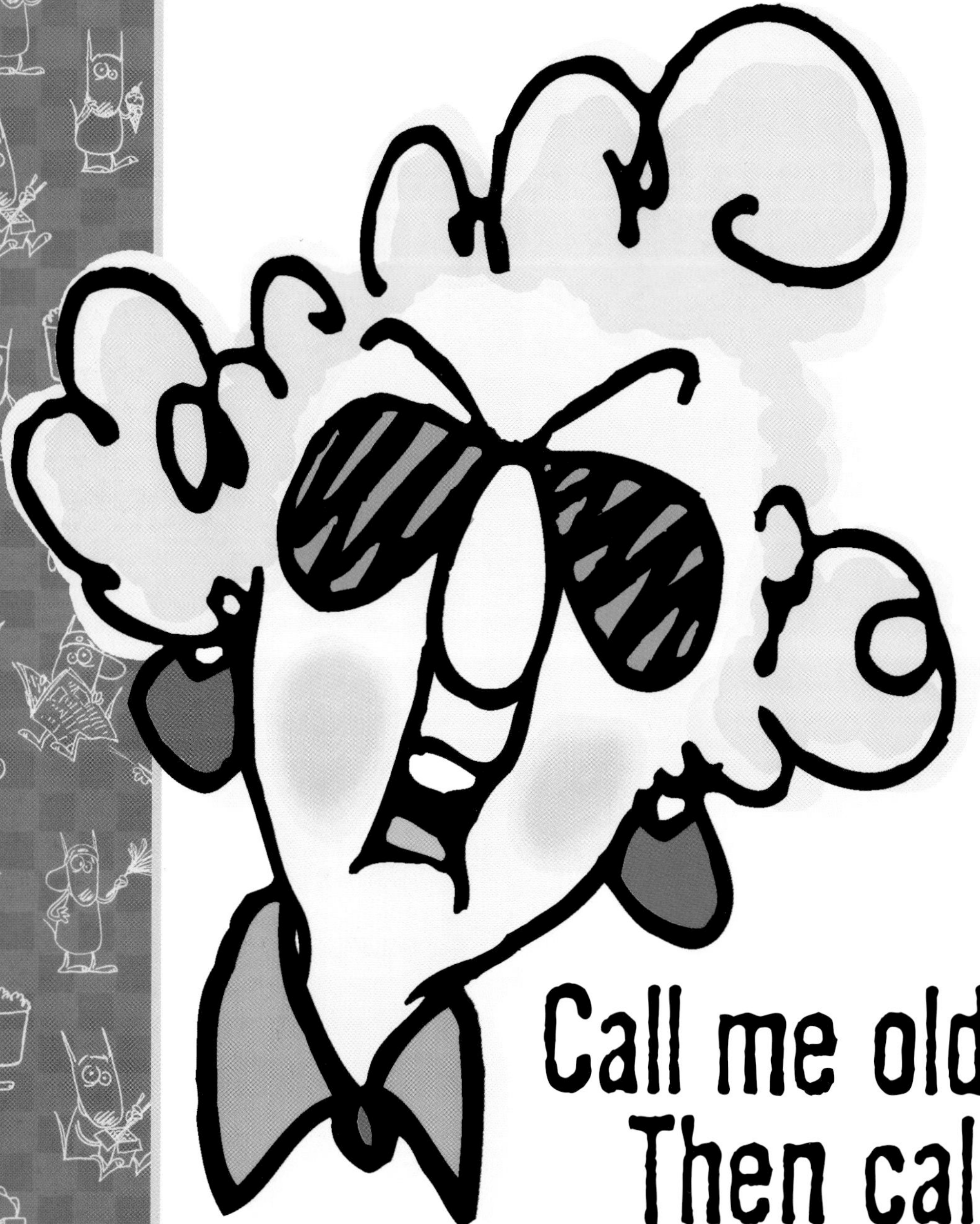

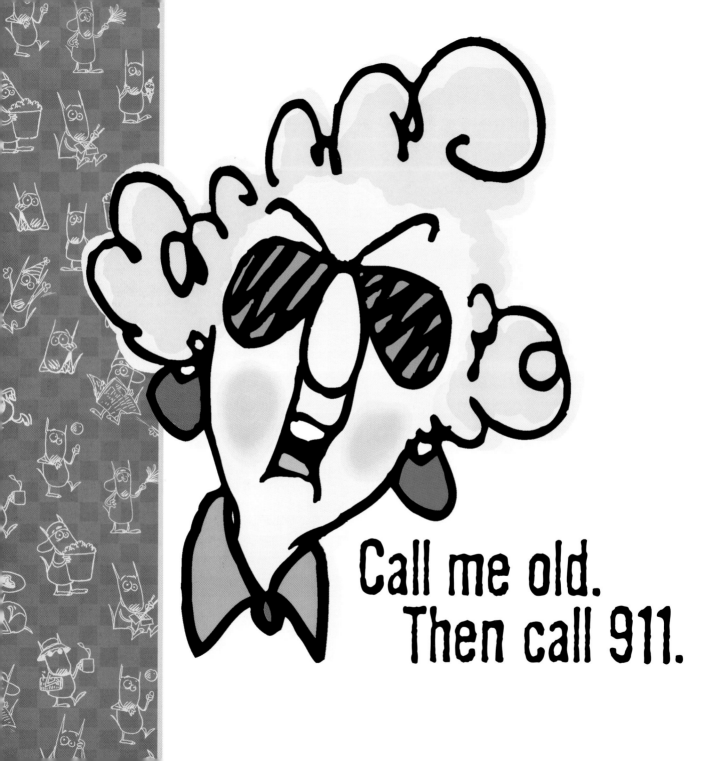

Call me old.
Then call 911.

Older But Wiseacre

COMPARED TO THE ALTERNATIVE, GETTING OLDER IS NOT A bad thing. The bad thing is having people (and I mean the people in charge of everything we read, see, and hear) so ready and willing to point it out to you.

Turn on the TV (which I'm prone to do no more than 12 or 13 hours a day), and you'll discover that people who know that big-band music doesn't mean three guitars are not exactly what advertisers call a desirable demographic. Apparently, no one buys a car or drinks a cola or votes or eats out or shops for laundry soap after they turn 23. We show up on family sitcoms for a few minutes to say something cranky or wacky and then head back to the basement or attic or, better yet, Florida.

I don't want to get on a soapbox, because frankly, I'm not crazy about heights. However, I must say that my years of experience have given me a body of wisdom bigger than a sumo wrestler on the Vegas Buffet Diet.

Older people made this country what it is. Should that be held against us? OK, maybe so. Forget I brought it up.

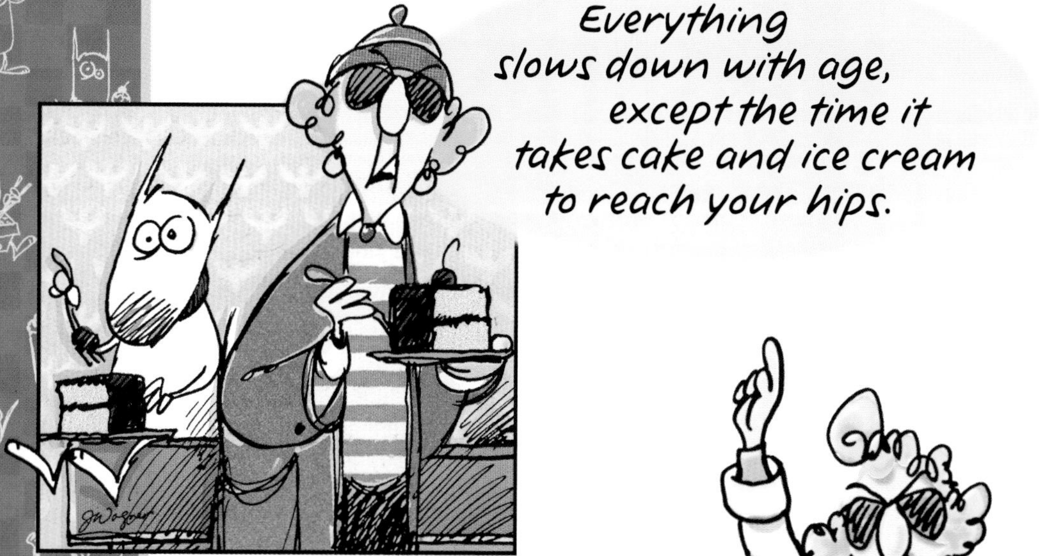
Everything slows down with age, except the time it takes cake and ice cream to reach your hips.

I used to have
Saturday Night Fever.
Now I just have
Saturday night
hot flashes.

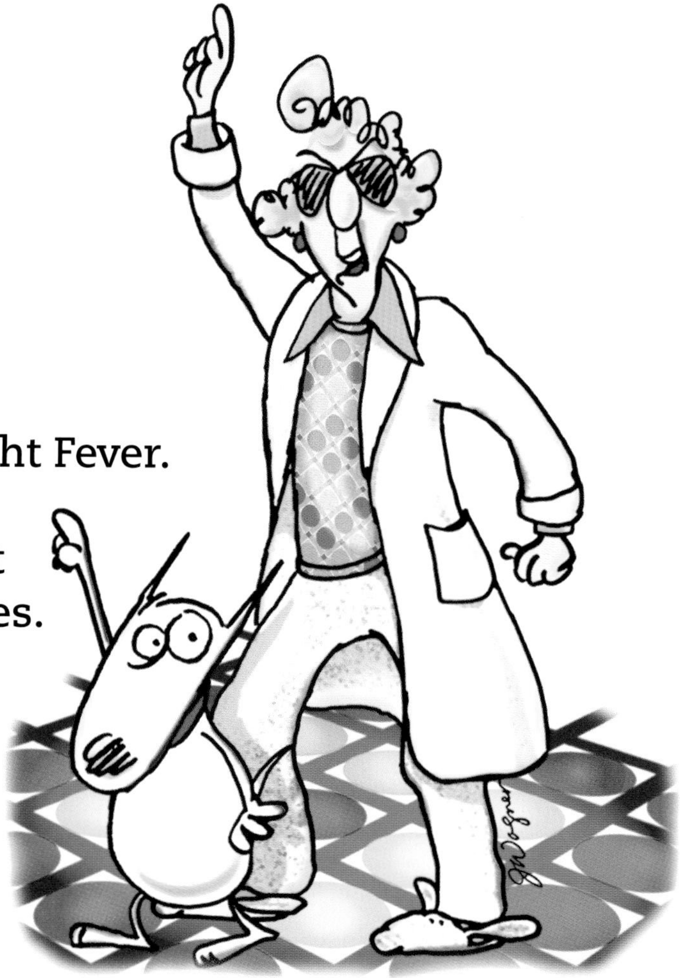

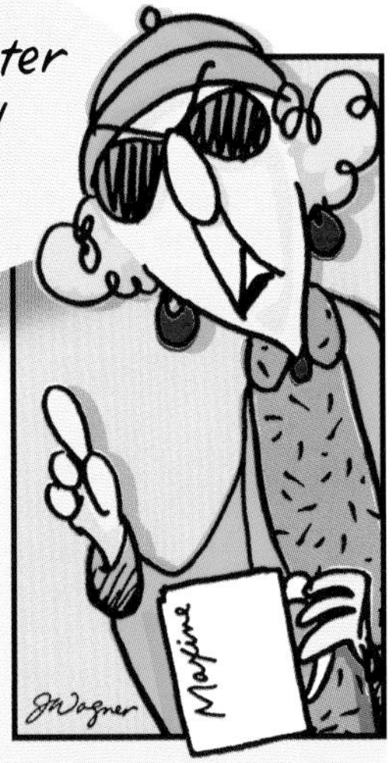
Actually, you can have a healthy sex life well into your later years. Assuming you can stand the sight of people your age naked.
Maxine

HERE'S ONE OF THE GREAT MYSTERIES OF life–nobody wants to think about their parents going at it, much less their grandparents, but by *definition,* we wouldn't be here if they hadn't. Just because there's snow on the roof, that doesn't mean there aren't a couple of sexy seniors underneath it doin' the adjustable-mattress mambo.

The tough thing about the wild thing is finding the time. Nobody's doing it in the morning. That's when you get your meds and check the paper to see who's still with us. Your stories aren't over until 2:00, and then the game shows come on, and before you know it, they're serving up the beef Stroganoff at the all-you-can-eat steam tray extravaganza.

Once the millionaire guy has gotten his final answer, it's time to call it a day...unless somebody's just gotten his Viagra. This drug makes penicillin look like moldy bread! Talk about a wonder drug! I wonder how anybody got along without it! Look for fishnet support hose and giant, underwire, lacy black bras at stores near you soon, and tell yourself your grandma's not buying them.

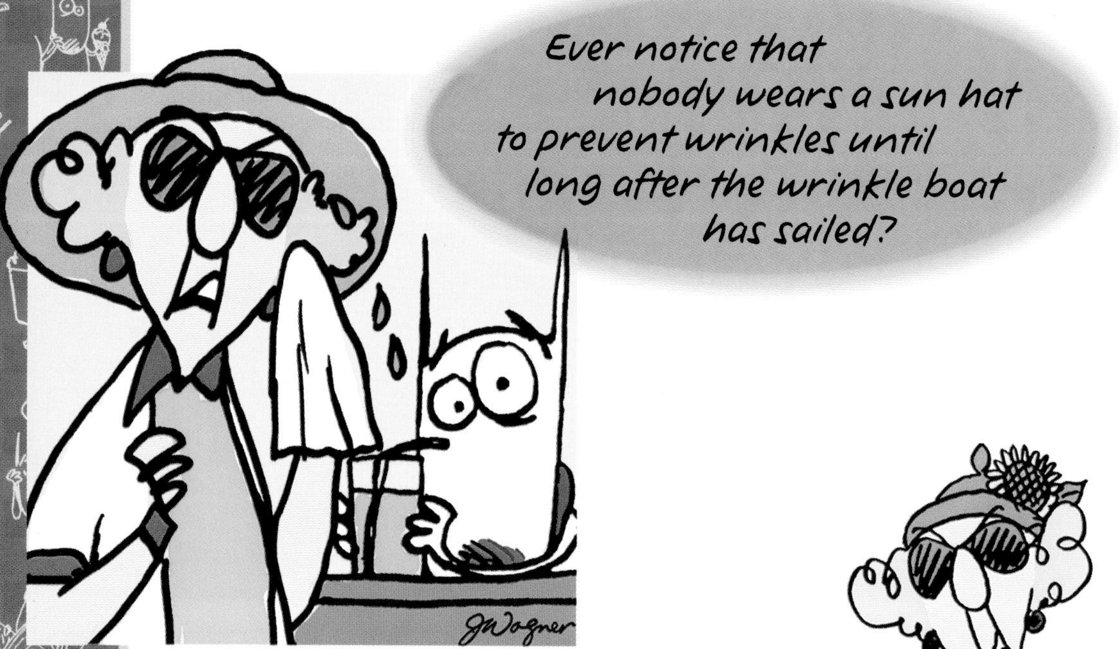
Ever notice that nobody wears a sun hat to prevent wrinkles until long after the wrinkle boat has sailed?
JWagner

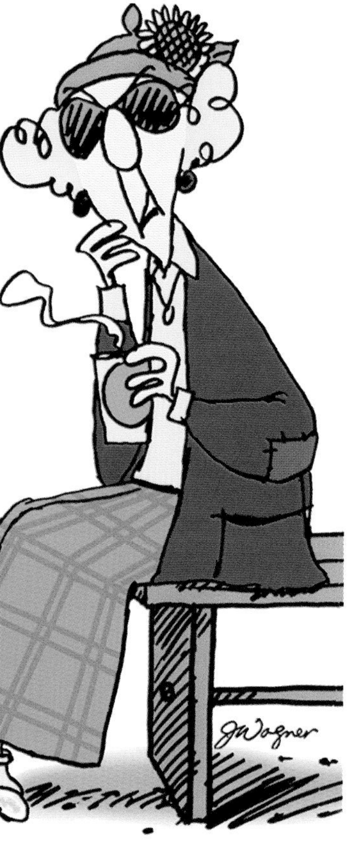
JWagner

At my age,
the bunny hop
is more like the
bunny shuffle.

Take every birthday
with a grain of salt.
This works much better if the
salt accompanies a large
margarita.

Mother Nature thinks of everything.
She makes our hair turn gray
before it falls out
so we don't miss
it as much.

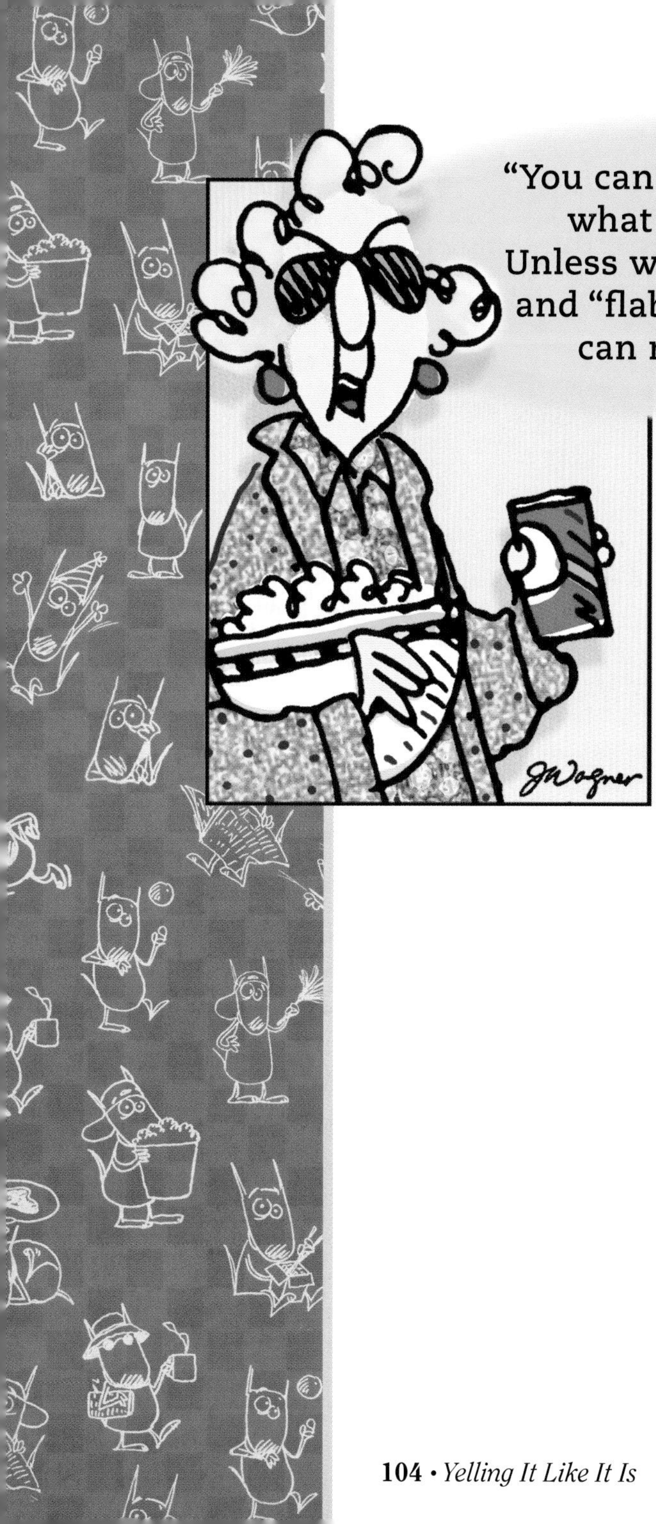

"You can't always get what you want." Unless what you want is "old" and "flabby." Most everyone can nail those two.

I may be old, but people who look like me always win the lottery.

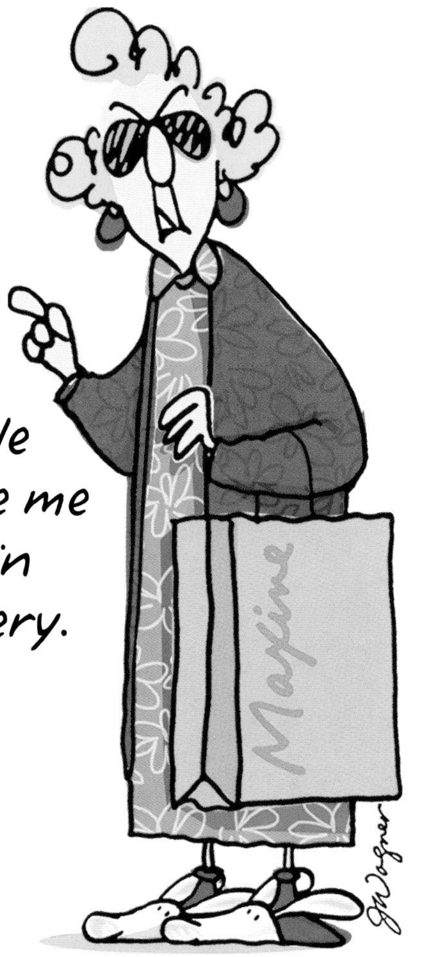
Maxine

A birthday is a good time to salute Father Time. Which finger you salute him with is your business.

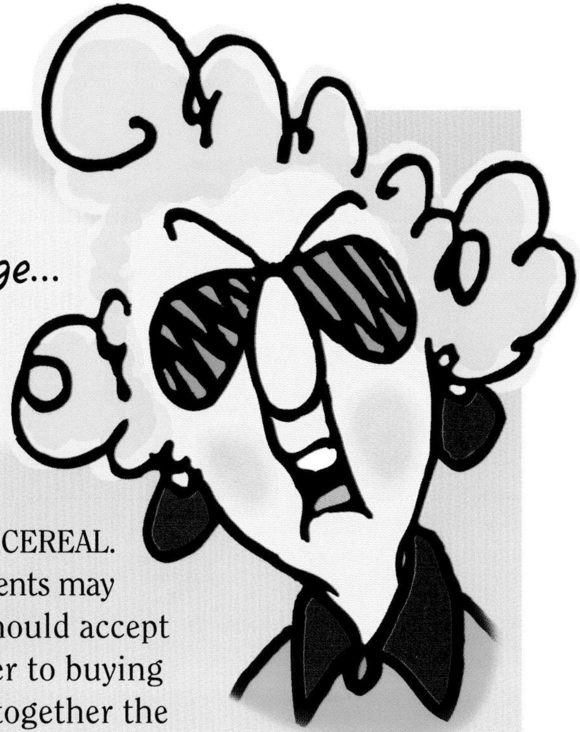
It's nice to see you doing so well at your age... you know, breathing and everything.

PEOPLE ARE LIKE BOXES OF CEREAL. In time, some settling of contents may occur. This is normal. We should accept it. Otherwise, we'll surrender to buying devices that painfully push together the parts that were meant to be strangers and prop up the parts that just want to lie down. I don't mind that I could start a fire by putting kindling between my thighs and walking around the block. I think of it as a hedge against the rising cost of home heating oil.

There are many advantages to getting older. Thinner hair dries faster. Looser skin catches more of the cool evening breeze. Fewer teeth means you save on dental floss.

Aging isn't so bad if you remember that not many of us were supermodels, and supermodels would kill to eat like us, so who really wins?

Never ask a lady her age. And don't ask me either.

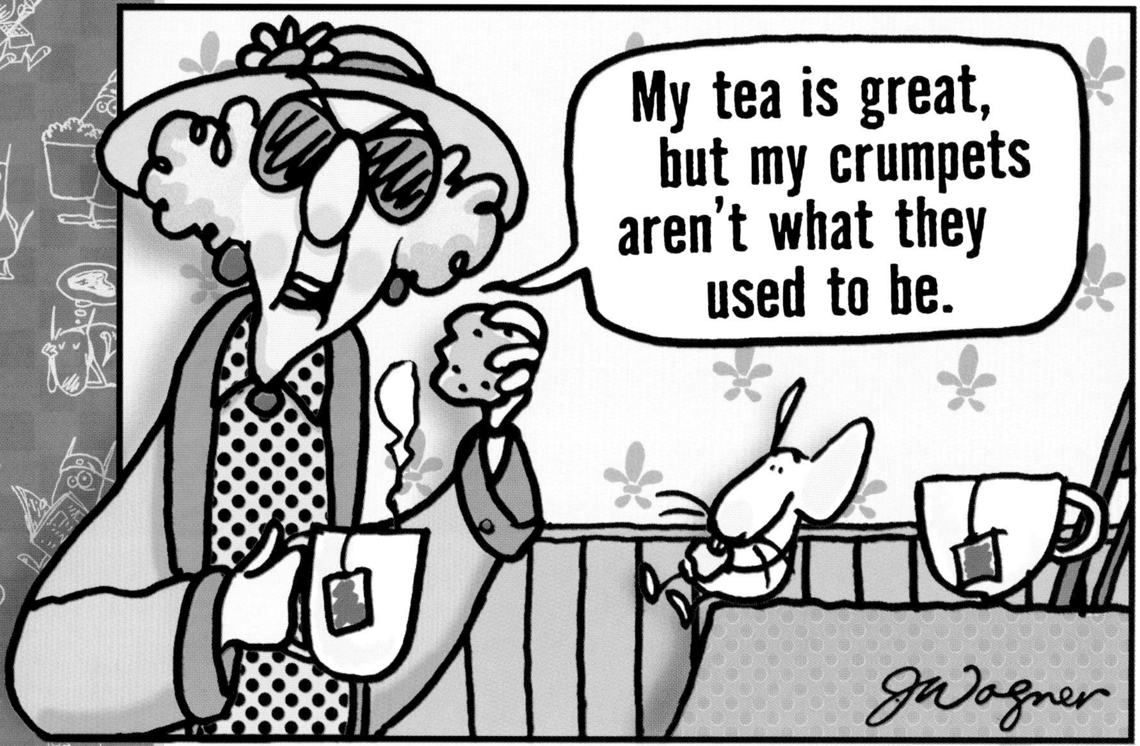
My tea is great, but my crumpets aren't what they used to be.
JWagner

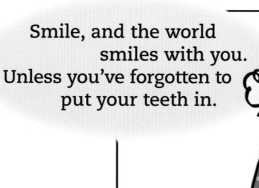

Smile, and the world smiles with you. Unless you've forgotten to put your teeth in.

Getting older? Well, no sense crying over spilled nutritional supplement.

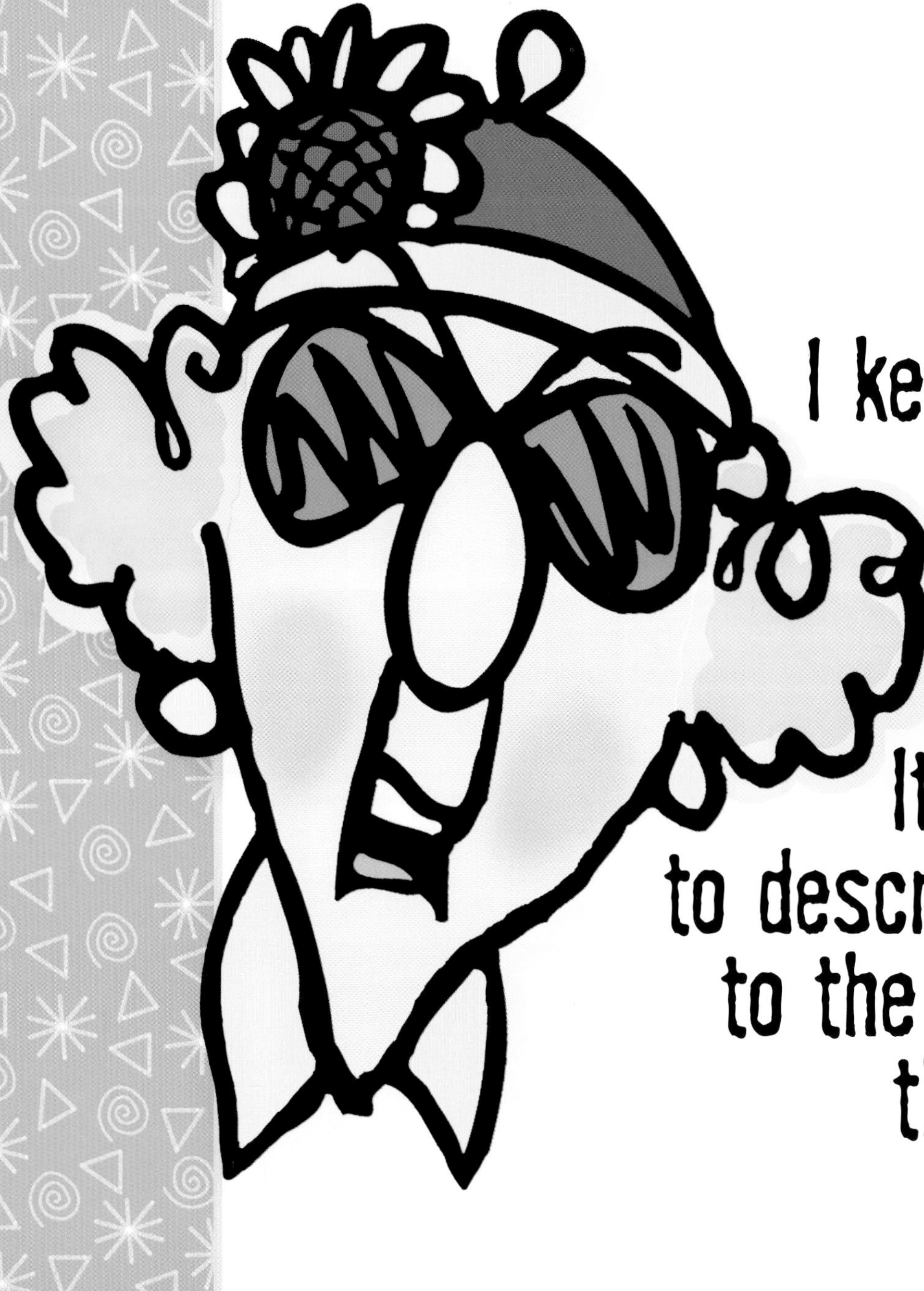

I keep lots of family photos on display. It's easier to describe them to the police that way.

The Family Scrappybook

JOHN WAGNER, THE WRITERS, AND MY DOG FLOYD HAVE become like family. Not in a good way. In fact, I'm not sure there *is* a good way.

John just couldn't try harder. He's very trying. I can't really blame him, though. It's not easy to capture all of this with a pen. Even with the endless stream of free ones he gets at work.

And speaking of people who nab free stuff at work, you won't find a store-bought paper clip in any writer's house. The writers and I get along well, because they make me sound good and I bring them unheard-of fame and adulation. Completely unheard of.

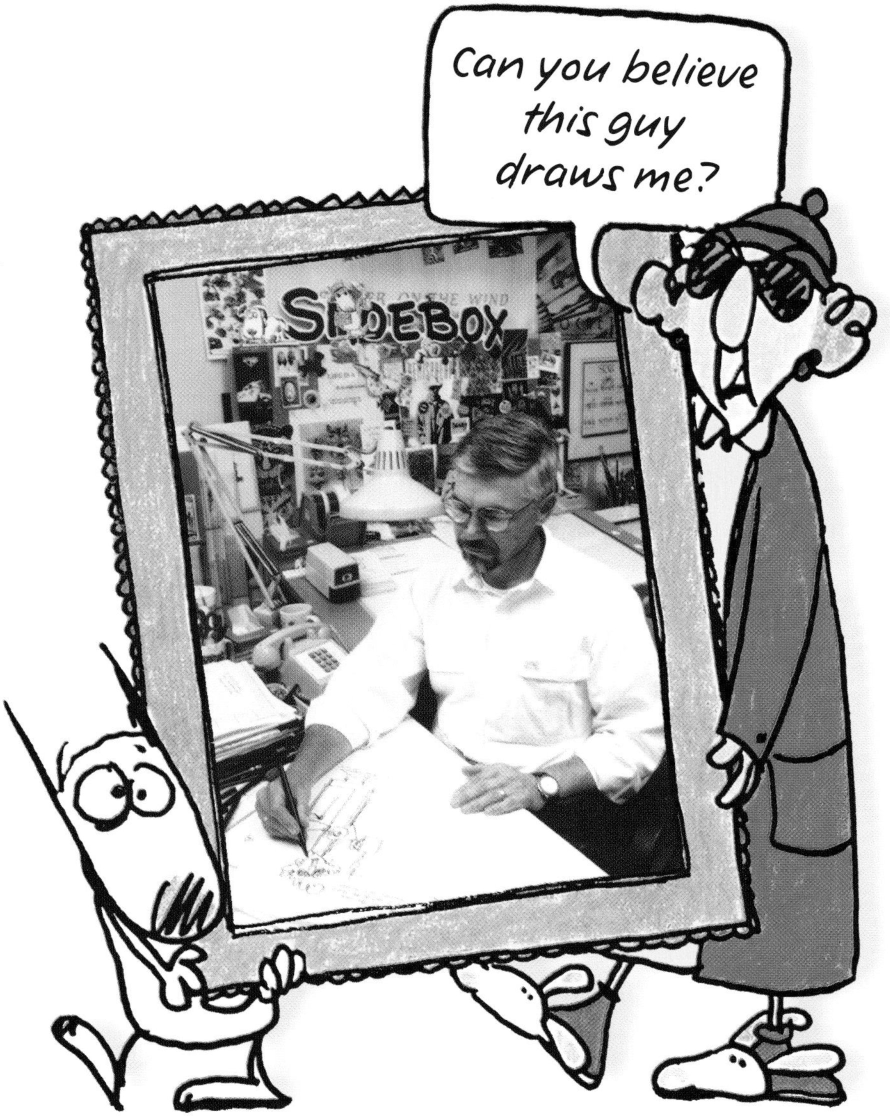
Can you believe this guy draws me?

John Wagner, creator of Maxine

IN THE LIFE OF EVERY GREAT ARTIST, THERE COMES a time when that great artist says, "Enough with sunsets and bowls of fruit, I want to draw something important!" That also happens to ham-fisted artists like John Wagner.

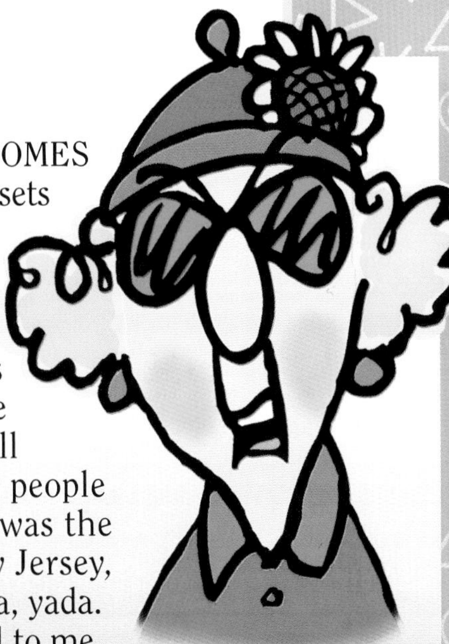

John first drew me in 1986. He says I'm a cross between his grandmother, his mother, and a couple of random aunts. Maybe that's why I'm so cross all the time. People find John fascinating. Especially people who don't know him. They love hearing that he was the third of nine children, he grew up in Leonia, New Jersey, he's been at Hallmark for over 30 years, yada, yada, yada. Thrilling information to some, surefire sleeping pill to me.

I've got a bone to pick with art boy. His drawings don't do me justice. I'm really what the whippersnappers call a "hot babe." The legs are too skinny, and the ol' housecoat isn't as filled out as it oughta be, if you know what I'm saying. Floyd is drawn accurately. So maybe it's easier to draw dogs. What do I know? I didn't go to art school. Not that it can be all that hard. What did John study at Vesper George School of Art in Boston? Intro to Doodling? Advanced Doodling? Principles of Anything Involving Nude Models?

Sometimes John has meetings with the writers so they can talk about what I'll do and say. It's sorta like the ants that crawl across Mt. Rushmore talking about national monuments. They might have opinions, but the main attraction ain't listening.

So the way it works is, John draws me and the writers come up with things for me to say. They're a team. A very successful team. A winning team. They're a team for the ages. Yeah, right, ages 3 to 5. I'm just kiddin'.

Here's some background information on the writers. Caution: This could result in excessive yawning.

THE WRITERS ARE A FASCINATING, brilliant, and almost ridiculously talented group. Of course, one of them must have written that, so, as I tell the waiter at Casa de Margaritas, take it with lots of grains of salt.

Seriously (and believe me, these writers, like writers everywhere, take themselves *way* too seriously), they're always coming up with clever, insightful, and just plain funny things for me to say. They do it by observing the world around them and seeing the funny side of the stuff we see all the time. It's not hard if you're a genius (there they go again—grab the salt shaker).

Now this is comedy!

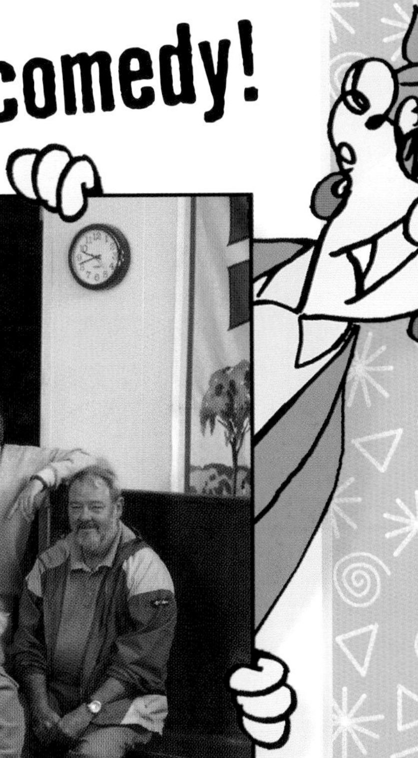

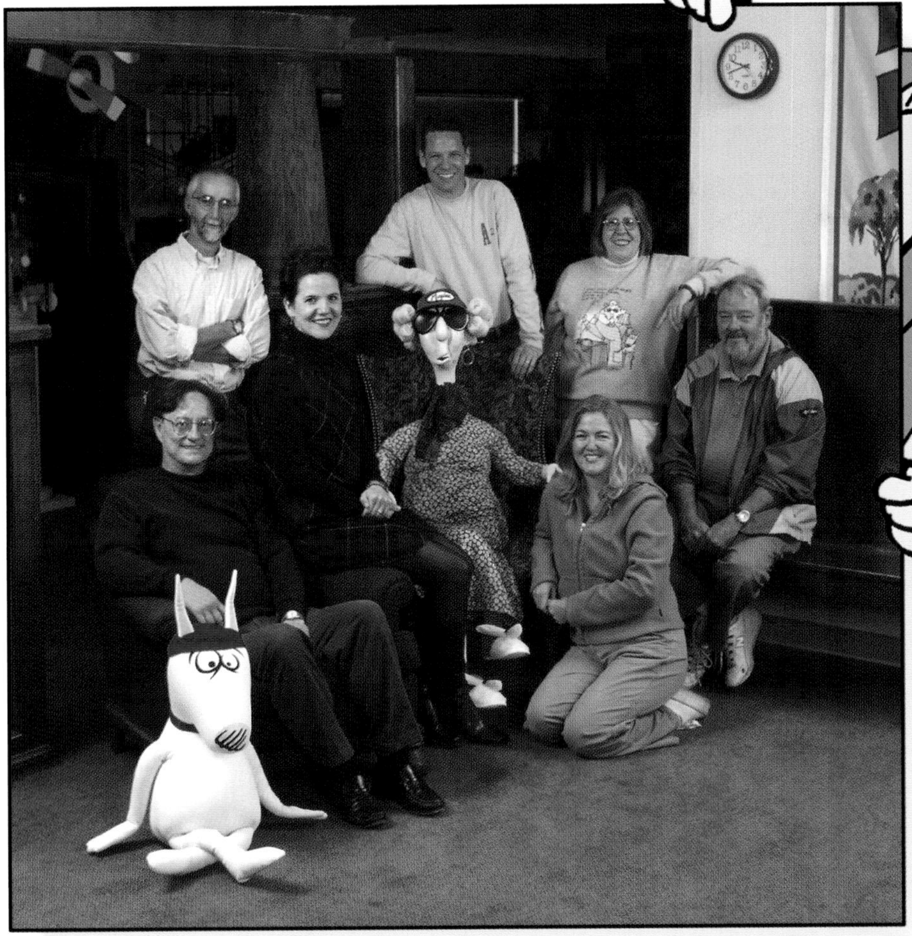

The crack staff of writers work long hours writing personal letters, grocery lists, and novels they'll never get published. And oh, yeah, occasionally they write a Maxine joke.

A FRIEND WHO never talks back, enthusiastically digs into whatever left-overs you're serving, and doesn't look better than you in the same outfit is a friend you want to hang on to. That's why Floyd is my amigo, my buddy, my pal, my... Hey! No dead birds in the kitchen! We've talked about this!

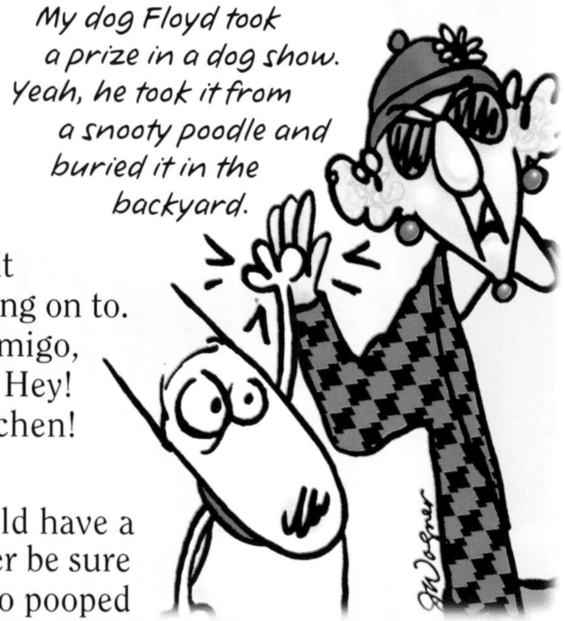
My dog Floyd took a prize in a dog show. Yeah, he took it from a snooty poodle and buried it in the backyard.

I think everyone should have a dog. That way, you'll never be sure that it was my pooch who pooped on your lawn. I, on the other finger, will be certain that yours soiled mine, and you'll hear about it. Dogs teach you about life. They are optimists–they see the toilet bowl as half-full. They also teach you that lots of things you never imagined eating are not only edible but apparently downright delicious. This includes, of course, any and all foods cooked in grease and the grease itself. Shoes and sofas are on the menu, too, and in a pinch, the Styrofoam your boneless chicken breasts came wrapped in. There isn't much your four-legged food processor won't eat and, in some cases, eat more than once.

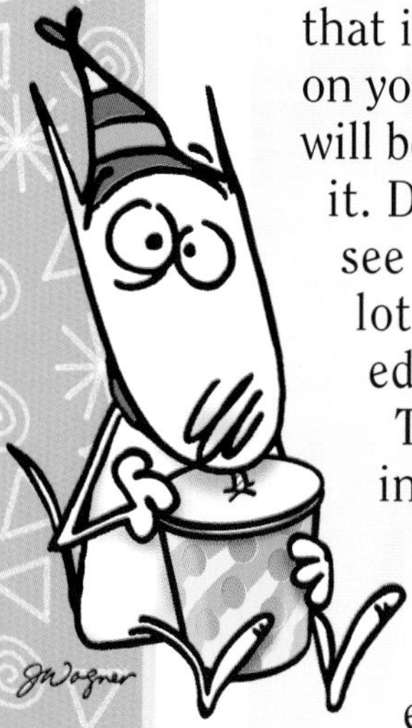

Floyd is an endless source of joy to me, and I wouldn't trade him for a handful of things I can think of off the top of my head, most of which I already have or don't really want.

He's a good watchdog. Especially when it comes to flies buzzing against a window-pane. He can watch for hours. I wouldn't say he's lazy, but instead of chasing the mailman, he just balls up his paw into a fist and shakes it at the guy.

He's smart, too. A poodle moved in down the street, and I'm almost sure I've noticed him barking with a French accent.

Floyd is the kind of dog most people only dream about. In that dream where they're being chased and chased by a goofy furry animal, and when they get to the bingo hall, they're naked. OK, maybe that's just me.

You're crabby? You're irritable? You swear you're one of my long-lost and lazy relatives? Skip the DNA test—take this quiz to find out. Answer these questions—then go score yourself!

Who Wants to Be an Old Blue Hair?

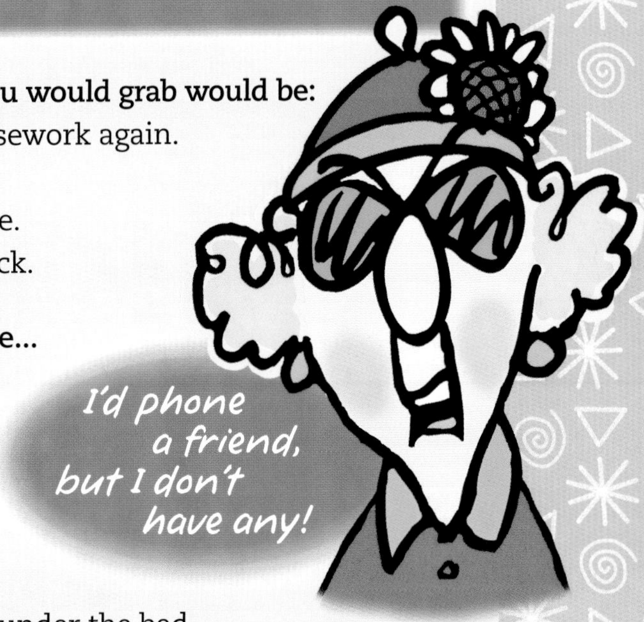
I'd phone a friend, but I don't have any!

1. If your house were on fire, the first thing you would grab would be:

(a) A nap, since you'll never have to do housework again.
(b) An alibi, for insurance purposes.
(c) Oven mitts, so you could save the remote.
(d) A bag of marshmallows and a pointy stick.

2. Finish this phrase: Early to bed, early to rise...

(a) Finish it yourself!
(b) Cuts down on the bloodshot eyes.
(c) Roll over and dream of throwing pies.
(d) You've got all day to criticize.

3. You think "spring cleaning" is:

(a) Enticing a longhaired cat to run around under the bed.
(b) What somebody ought to do to the springs.
(c) What somebody ought to do to the wall where the pie hit it.
(d) A waste of time, since the house might burn down, anyway.

Scoring:

All "a": You're not a relative, but you're relatively lazy!
All "b": We're not family, but you're sneaky, suspicious, and my kind of person.
All "c": You may be a distant cousin, so keep your distance!
All "d": Better add you to the family tree! You're wearing bunny slippers and a housecoat right now, aren't you?

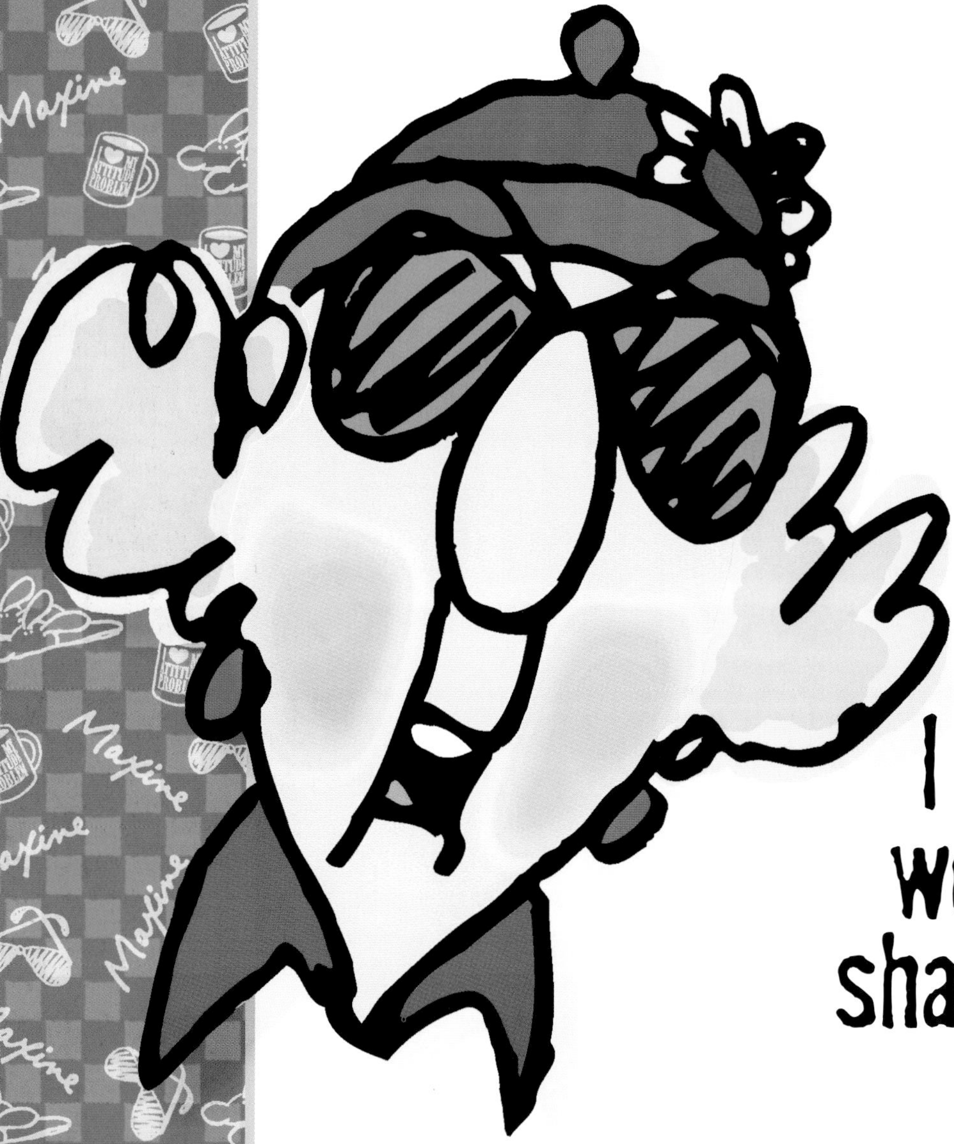

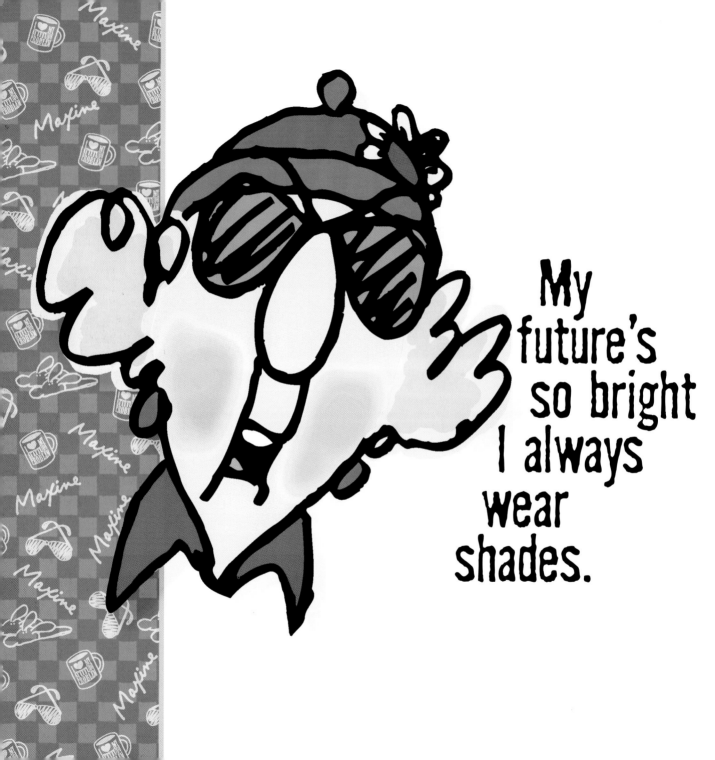

My
future's
so bright
I always
wear
shades.

Eat My Slipper Dust

WHERE WILL I GO NEXT? WHAT WILL I DO NEXT? THESE are questions for my parole officer. Just kidding. I don't really mind the community service, anyway. Who doesn't want cleaner roadsides?

Seriously, my future's so bright I always wear shades. Teams of experts are working around their many extended breaks to come up with new adventures and exciting vistas for themselves. Then, when the boss walks by, they spring into action for yours truly.

Look for me on the small screen...or maybe the big screen if you've got one of those monolithic altars to entertainment in your living room. Then there's always the movies. Wonder if stars get some kind of senior discount on popcorn...

Hmmm…maybe I'll buy my own cruise line.
Kind of a "No-Love-Lost Boat."

You can
be"King of
the World" on
my cruise line,
but don't try
to boss me
around.

Or I might start my own restaurant chain
called MAXINE'S CRABBY CAFÉ –
"Where the line between toasted and burnt is very thin."

Would you
like that...
well,
I don't care
how you'd
like that.

You know what I'd be good at?
Writing my own advice column. It would give me a chance
to say in print what I usually say under my breath.

Maxine's Crabby Corner

The world is going to hell in an SUV, and whoever is driving is too busy talking on a cell phone to notice.

I reached this conclusion after a visit this morning to my neighborhood gas station/convenience store/gouge-a-torium.

Now, I've been driving for quite a while. My first car was two stone wheels and a stick, so I'm old enough to remember when a team of smiling attendants rushed out to check my oil, check my water, check my tires. Heck, on a good day, they even checked me out.

Now everything's self-serve. I don't know how you feel, but I'm not the kind of person I particularly want to be served by.

After shoving my credit card into the pump every way but folded in half, I finally got the request to choose which kind of gas I wanted—the cheapest, the kind that was a nickel more a gallon, or the kind that was a dime more a gallon. Hmmm...that's a poser.

As the gas tinkled into the tank, I realized that nature was calling. Well, screaming, actually. I went inside to use the "clean, comfortable" rest room. Trust me, friends. I know clean and comfortable. Clean and comfortable are friends of mine. This rest room was not clean and comfortable.

I half expected to see John Hancock's signature on the "Last cleaned by..." sheet.

Holding my breath and attempting to levitate over the seat, one thing was suddenly clear–the reason they keep the rest rooms locked is not to keep people out, it's to keep mutating fungi in.

As I transacted my business, I read the graffiti. Apparently, you can have a good time by calling someone named Bob. Do you suppose that ever works? Is there a couple somewhere celebrating their golden anniversary and she's saying "We met when I saw Bob's number on a gas station rest room wall. So I called him, and you know what? He really WAS a good time!"

I washed my hands and waited next to the hot-air dryer. And waited. And waited. I'm thinkin' they should just include "Wipe Hands on Pants" as the final instruction on those things.

"Hey, Junior," I said to the kid reading the hot rod magazine behind the counter. "The hand dryer in the ladies' room is busted. You need to either have a working bathroom or stop sellin' quart-size slushies."

When he looked at me with a blank expression and answered "Huh?" I knew the problem would soon be taken care of.

"Hand dryer," I repeated. "Ladies' room. Broken. Stop me if this is too complex for you."

"Want me to get the manager?" he mumbled.

"Oh, no. I wouldn't want to interrupt his junior high classes."

"Yeah, right," Mr. Efficient answered. "He's in high school."

I paid a buck for a nickel's worth of candy bar and headed back out into the fume-laden sunshine.

After all, rush hour traffic was waiting.

Maxine
Get out of my space.

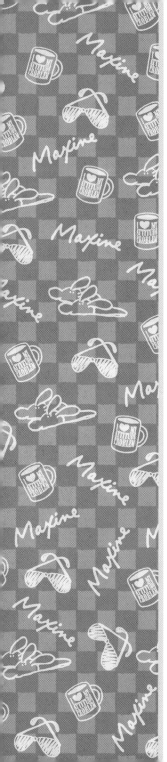

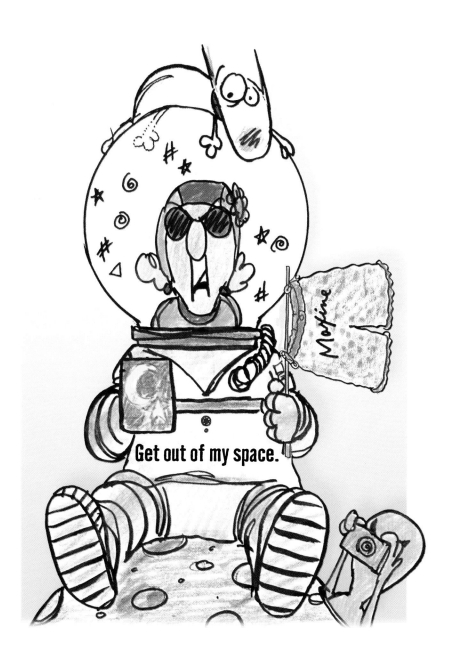

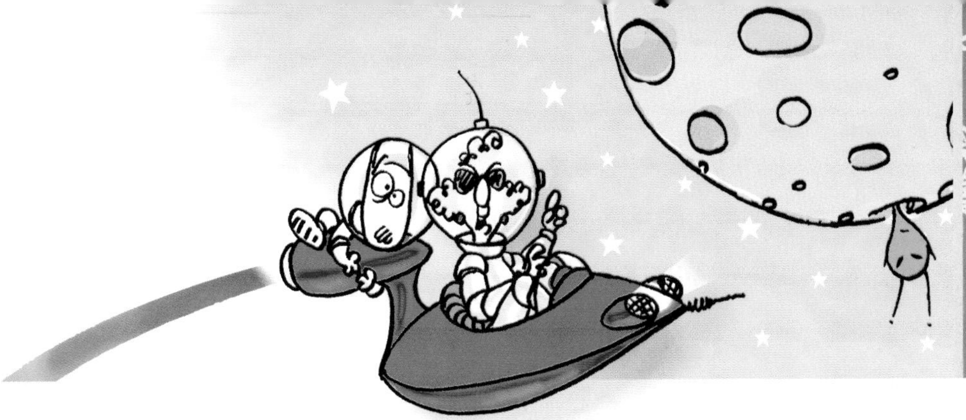

THE SKY'S THE LIMIT. OR IS IT? I CAN SEE MYSELF LEADING THE FIRST colony of settlers on the moon. Oh, it'd be tough at first, but through hard work and dedication, I believe the simple folk would learn to worship me.

In the lessened gravity, it'd be easy (and fun!) to build many giant statues of me, and maybe one of Floyd while they're at it. A statue in an oxygen-free environment where pigeons can't live–something everyone dreams of!

My reign would be like my butt. Firm but fair. A little better than "fair," if I say so myself. I'd rule with an iron finger, but I'd listen to the little guy. I wouldn't have to do anything he said, because he's little, but I'd listen.

And when we inevitably went to war with Mars, I'd lead the attack. In principle. From my luxurious bunker deep under the lunar surface. I'd follow the reports closely and try to remember the names of the generals or whatever.

You say this sounds crazy–I say there goes your appointment to a cushy position on the moon-rock collection team, sucker!

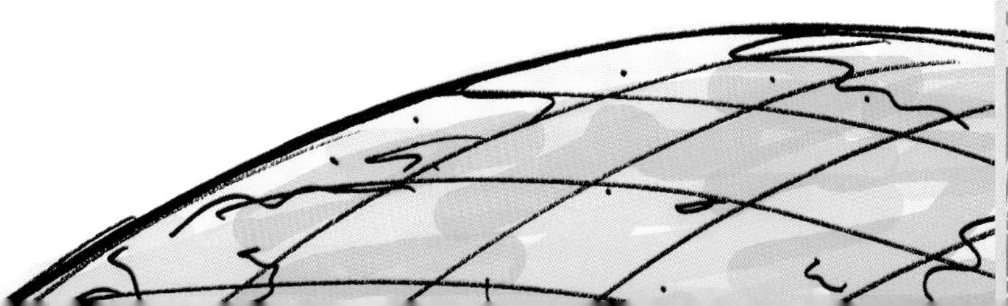